Downers Grove Public Library
1050 Curtiss St.
Downers Grove, IL 60515

Emilie Schindler

WHERE LIGHT AND SHADOW MEET

A Memoir

W · W · NORTON & COMPANY

NEW YORK  LONDON

Emilie Schindler

WHERE

WITH ERIKA ROSENBERG

LIGHT AND

TRANSLATED FROM

SHADOW

THE ORIGINAL SPANISH BY

MEET

DOLORES M. KOCH

A MEMOIR

For information about permission to reproduce selections from
this book, write to Permissions,
W. W. Norton & Company, Inc., 500 Fifth Avenue,
New York, NY 10110.

The text of this book is composed in 11/13.5 Fairfield LH Light
with the display set in Lucian BT Roman
Desktop composition by David Gilbert, Wildman Productions
Manufacturing by The Haddon Craftsmen, Inc.
Book design by Margaret M. Wagner

Library of Congress Cataloging-in-Publication Data

Schindler, Emilie, 1907-
[Memorias. English]
Where light and shadow meet : a memoir / Emilie Schindler with
Erika Rosenberg ; translated by Dolores M. Koch.
   p.   cm.
ISBN 0-393-04123-9
1. Schindler, Emilie, 1907– . 2. World War, 1939–1945—Personal
narratives, Czech. 3. Schindler, Oskar, 1908–1974. 4. World War,
1939–1945—Jews—Rescue. 5. Righteous Gentiles in the Holocaust—
Biography. I. Rosenberg, Erika. II. Title.
D811.5.S31513   1997
940.53'18'092—dc21
[B]   96-49019
                                                                CIP

W. W. Norton & Company, Inc., 500 Fifth Avenue, New York, N.Y. 10110
http://www.wwnorton.com

W. W. Norton & Company Ltd., 10 Coptic Street, London WC1A 1PU

1234567890

Contents

Acknowledgments

EMILIE SCHINDLER AND ERIKA ROSENBERG WISH TO thank Mr. and Mrs. Bernhard Scheuer, as well as Dr. J. Bedsky, for their longtime friendships that have overcome all distances. And to the B'nai B'rith Foundation for their support through difficult moments.

We want to express our special gratitude also to Marcos Mayer, for all his efforts to make this memoir available to readers.

To Peter Apelt of the Buenos Aires Goethe Institute, and to Alvaro and Hernán Gutiérrez Zaldívar, for their unconditional support and indispensable encouragement.

Finally, to Eric and José Rosenberg, to the memory of Adela and Benno Band, and to all those who by their example were sources of inspiration for the writing of this memoir.

Prologue

From the Other Side of the World

SOME OF YOU WILL GENEROUSLY FORGIVE ME IF MY story is not precisely what you expected, but I trust that, in the end, you will thank me for not lying to you. I am writing from the edge where light and shadow meet. That is my only gift. Oskar Schindler was bathed in all the light that history accorded him, and I feel that is not entirely fair. I am doing this not for him but for the sake of truth. People should know how these events actually took place.

Steven Spielberg's film, Thomas Keneally's book, and all the rivers of ink spilled fifty years after the facts depict my husband as a hero for this century. This is not true. He was not a hero, and neither was I. We only did what we had to. In times of war our souls wander aimlessly adrift. I was one of those fleeting shadows affected by atrocity, by all its misery and vehemence, suspicion and contradiction, which have left an indelible mark in my memory. It's all here, within my head, no longer painful. . . . Or is it? Perhaps I am too old to allow myself the consolation of pain. Old age also brings us a kind of relief, with its shadows and its apathy. Nothing is urgent now. I am speaking of times past, and once in a while I let the present intrude and distract me.

In one hour the year 1994 will come to an end. Someone sitting at my side reminds me how much the world has changed in recent times: all of Germany is finally reunited, there is talk of peace between Jews and Arabs, and the Soviet Union has crumbled. . . . But violence has not subsided: hatred still flourishes. Serbs and Bosnians are dying in a war that seems to threaten all of Europe. Terrorist attacks are on the increase, in Washington, Paris, and Buenos Aires. In such a short period of time so much has happened that at present we find ourselves thrown into deep uncertainty, while the past seems forever destined to oblivion. Nothing is as it appears to be, even though on a night like this everybody's gaze is focused only on the future.

Friends sharing my dinner table do not stop praising the simple fare that I prepared for them. The festive spirit is in harmony with their hopes for the year about to begin. Suddenly someone comes out of the kitchen and proposes a toast. His head hits the crystal chandelier, a present from Francisco Wichter, the only "Schindler's list" survivor living in Argentina. Everyone screams, fearing that he has hurt himself. What draws my attention at the moment, however, is the swaying of the crystal chandelier, and its continuous shifting of light and shadow. My mind wanders watching it sway; at no time do I fear that the whole thing might be knocked down. It is firmly secured to the ceiling and others have bumped into it before. This chandelier, much like me, has had its share of hard knocks. I hung it myself at that particular height because I am short now and there is no longer a risk of my knocking it down. Perhaps when I was younger, and my height not yet shortened by infirmity, I was one of those who, when moving forward, would knock some high things down.

Until recently I rarely had visitors. So far away from it all, so far away from the world. . . . The swaying of the crystal chandelier mesmerizes me, and I follow its fringes in their pendular movement. I disengage from those around me, and I feel they would not be here if someone had not thought of unearthing my husband's—Oskar Schindler's—life story and that of the Plaschow concentration camp. That is, the rescue of more than a thousand Jews at a time when death was their clear and inevitable fate. All this is on the side of light. And what about the shadows? That is the side I have grown accustomed to, like a little girl who has lost her way in the forest and does not know how to find her way back home. I ask myself whether it is worthwhile to come out of the shadows. Someone might say, "Emilie, these are old stories." But are they really? Scenes from Spielberg's film cross my mind, struggling to overshadow the real memories. I resist, and I look again at the faces of those around me. The chandelier has stopped swaying. We are in the realm of light again.

The satisfied faces of my guests, though, conjure up as if in a dream other distant and nameless faces. I see the eyes of those workers, the Jewish workers in the ammunition factory Oskar and I ran toward the end of 1944 at Brünnlitz, a small Czechoslovakian town. . . . I have seen them again, now grown old, in Argentina, in Miami, in Palm Beach, and in New York. They recognized me and greeted me, but I could neither remember their names nor recognize their faces. A very fragile, stooped woman approached me in Los Angeles to thank me in a trembling voice for a chocolate bar that I had given her almost half a century ago. Faces appear out of the shadows to bring me the belated rewards of those moments fraught with death.

The ghosts from those times have never left me: they still follow me closely. One thing becomes clear to me on this New Year's Eve, while the noise and the bursts of light from the fireworks seem to take over everything, and the warm weather reminds me of it: that I live on the other side of the world, thousands of miles from the place where I was born. . . . As I think of the past, images of my childhood and of my family home keep coming back. A deep sadness comes over me. And yet, I smile. Tonight I no longer feel alone. I have decided to write my story, to share it with the world, in the same way that during the war I struggled to share bread and shelter with "my Jews," if I may still refer to them that way.

I am going to tell you my story. It is all I have. I will not portray Oskar as a hero. I have loved him, I have hated him, I have tried to forget him. . . . I have lived by his side and under his shadow, but I had my own light, just like the crystal chandelier swaying tonight, which is perhaps trying to tell me something. This chandelier was my only companion in those times when no one knew of my existence, when I tried to survive without a past, without memories.

I know that the decision to write my memoir means I have to immerse myself again in the shadows, though this time in the hope of finding the light again, of making my peace with the world, with history, with the truth. To be Emilie again, simply Emilie.

Writing is exhausting. That is what my body tells me, what my bones complain about. I look at my hands, all wrinkled and withered, but still strong enough to hold on to my cane and to my pen. I am going to leave my thoughts for a moment and return to the party. I celebrate and secretly thank God that I am still granted the time.

Note: There have been some minor changes to the original, approved by the authors. Added information has been indicated within brackets. Readers familiar with Keneally's Schindler's List, *please note that he used Polish spelling for many place-names, while Emilie Schindler used Czech or German spelling.—DMK*

PART ONE

Childhood in Bohemia

Under the Sign of Libra

I WASN'T ALWAYS EMILIE SCHINDLER. MY FAMILY name is Pelzl, which in German means "fur," from which I assume that my ancestors were hunters. I was born on October 22, 1907, under the sign of Libra, in the city of Alt Moletein, in the earldom of Hohenstadt. My family had settled in that region in the twelfth century, when Bohemia was part of the German Empire and ruled by Ottocar II, the greatest representative of the Premysl dynasty.

As far as I know, my ancestors came to Moravia as settlers. Their history was recorded on an old family genealogical passport that disappeared, together with so many other valuable items, in the chaos of war during our flight from Brünnlitz.

In my native city, like everywhere else in the world, there was an upper class and a lower class. The upper class included the doctors and the civil servants, the clergy and the teachers; the lower class, the poor, included the laborers or field hands who helped with the harvest or tilled the fertile soil. The town was elongated in shape and densely populated, with a fairly old church in its

Rothwasser
Halda
Plana
Hertersdorf
Jokelsdorf
Nepomuk
Chaudoba
Johnsdorf
Schönwald
Pirkelsdorf
Moletein
Neu
Charlottendf.
Seibelsdf.
Moletein
Annabad
Ziegenfuss
Türpes
Reichenau
Trieb
Kl. Hermigsdf.
Rehsdorf
Stillfried
Kunzendorf
Dittersdorf
Neudorf
Hohenfeld
Altstadt
Tschuschitz
Mähr.
Ketzelsdorf
Undangs
Bhf.
Schönhengst
Mähr. Triba
Böhm
Lussdorf
Budigsdf
Sichelsdf
Tattenitz

*This small dot on the map of Bohemia is
Alt Moletein, my place of birth.*

center, an army post, a market square, a hospital and several schools, an important library, and a long history of war battles and old traditions, evident at every corner.

We were comfortably well-off. Our house had been renovated during the past century, although in truth it was an old dwelling built by Swedes, who had occupied the region in the early 1700s.

There were not many of us Pelzls: my parents, my brother Franz, and my paternal grandparents, who had their own house in the middle of a large farm. My family home was roomy and comfortable, as country houses tend to be. My parents worked hard and had managed to build some capital. We grew mainly flax, wheat, and rye, and in our wonderful orchard we had a variety of fruit trees surrounded by beautiful flowers of different sizes and intense colors, my father's pride and joy.

The image of my grandmother, with whom I spent most of my time, fills the memories of my childhood. The old woman paid a seamstress to make clothes especially for me and worried about my eating right, something I steadfastly resisted. No matter what dishes or delicacies were served, I often refused to take even a bite.

One day, when my grandmother tried to force-feed me, I got scared and ran into the garden with a piece of bread I had stolen from the table and climbed to the top of a cherry tree. Somewhat thoughtlessly and somewhat satisfied with myself, I enjoyed the view of the world from up there, and I devoured the bread and helped myself to the cherries on the tree.

Even in such childish and inconsequential pranks, I started to show the stubbornness that was to stay with me for the rest of my life and that I have never regretted, because it helped me survive whenever the road seemed to be blocked ahead of me.

A Look at the Horses

ON THE ALT MOLETEIN FAMILY FARM WE ALSO RAISED ANIMALS: chickens, geese, ducks, goats, cows, horses, and, of course, cats and dogs. Life went on peacefully and without economic worries.

At the age of three I was already going with my parents to the fields. Nature, ever since then, has held a magical attraction for me. Even today I am drawn to the television screen whenever I see a rural setting.

On one such outing, I had the opportunity to observe the underside of a horse. . . .

While my father was plowing the land with his two horses one morning, I managed to quickly slide unnoticed under one of them.

My father whistled, and right away the horse started to move, but realizing I was underneath, it slowed down, neighed loudly, and balked.

The horse did not want to hurt me. I felt safe where I was, looking at its golden belly and muscular legs, until my father dragged me out, complaining about my insatiable curiosity. This incident intensified my love for horses, those fabulous creatures endowed with such extraordinary sensitivity. They were my friends and part of an environment in which everything seemed destined to protect me.

My mother was a very understanding, adorable woman who always found an affectionate and appropriate word for those around her. We all knew that we could count on her unconditional affection and sympathy. She used to ask me to help her with the many household chores and give me a small allowance, which I saved in a spirit of prudence and thrift. Aside from such rewards, I really enjoyed farm work. I did not, however, devote as much effort as I should have to the long and boring piano lessons that I was forced to take, since I completely lacked any ear or vocation for music.

The discovery of the natural environment placed me in such close contact with living creatures, with everything that pulsated and renewed itself, that I never paid any attention to dolls or any other kinds of toys. I preferred animals and plants, anything that was alive and moved, and especially horses, my very dear friends.

Gypsy Tales

AS I WAS GROWING UP, I CAME TO REALIZE THAT SOME PEOPLE differed from us. One day I went to town with my mother to sell farm eggs, and I saw seated at a bar some thin, dark-skinned men with raven-black hair and dark eyes. I noticed their way of dressing and especially that of their women, which was showy and vividly colorful.

Gypsies have attracted me since I was a child. I loved to watch their faces, with their olive complexion and the rare intensity of their shining, jet-black eyes. I admired their free and independent way of life, not tied to any kind of conventionalism. So every time they came to town, where they were allowed to remain for only five days, and then at a predetermined site, I used to go by, talk with them, and listen to their songs and their tales, which transported me to all those marvelous places they had been in their eternal wandering.

I could never figure out why Gypsies were regarded and treated with so much apprehension. My mother provided me with some information about them, and soon I was investigating their origins and customs. Their nomadic and free spirit, so removed from what I had seen in the rest of society, captivated me then and forever.

Since I spent so much time with them, one day in an old abandoned granary, a Gypsy woman who used to come often to Alt Moletein read my palms. She was fat, had a sallow complexion, brown eyes, and heavy braids. Her skirt was wide, and she wore a vest with golden arabesques over a lilac-colored muslin blouse. Although from my childish perspective she appeared to be enormous, her voice sounded higher than I had expected and, at the same time, grave. She looked me squarely in the eye and announced that she was going to tell me my future. And taking my hands in hers, she said:

"I see, child, that your lifeline is long. You will have a long life, longer than you think. But you will also experience much pain and suffering. You will meet a man who will take you away from here. You will love him above all, although you will not be happy at his side. I also see other people around you, but I do not know who they are or what they are doing. There are other things, my child, that I do not dare tell you."

The face of the Gypsy woman suddenly darkened. I was scared, very scared. In tears, I ran outside the granary, and I buried myself in my mother's lap. She had begun to worry about my absence and asked me again and again where I had been. But I was not brave enough to tell her the truth. I have jealously kept it a secret all my life, and I only told Oskar during our long trip to Argentina.

"Emilie," he said, hugging me, "you can no longer believe in these things and go on torturing yourself. If you have not been happy up to now, I will see to it that you are in the future. You can be sure that I love you."

The Gypsy woman, however, did know what she was saying. She had seen the truth, she had read it in my hands. And the predicted misfortunes proved accurate not only for me but also for her own people. Not enough has been said about the brutal treatment Gypsies suffered under the Nazis, and how they were almost wiped out from the European continent.

My Father's Silence

IN 1914, WHEN I WAS JUST STARTING TO DISCOVER THE WORLD, the war broke out. I was scarcely seven years old, and from that terrible experience I was able to perceive only feelings of sadness and anxiety, which deepened considerably when my father was called into the service.

The day he left I sensed that nothing would ever be the same. While he was away, we had to struggle hard to keep the farm going, and in my loneliness our animals and the forest were of great comfort to me. I used to spend a good part of the day in the forest, looking at the huge pine trees, the ancient oaks, and the exuberant birches, which seemed to huddle together as if keeping each other company. The birds were warbling up among the branches, and their songs sounded to my young ears like greetings from afar, from beyond the heavens.

Coming out of the prevailing semidarkness, those sounds and images, and the delicate scent of the pine cones scattered about on the soft ground, enthralled me to the point that more than once I truly believed that the forest was enchanted. This feeling was strongest in winter, when the branches were covered by a solid whiteness and the snow crunched under my feet. In those magical surroundings, I felt like the only guest invited to the celebration.

At nightfall, alone in my bed, I thought of my father and felt that the war was taking too long. But one day it was over. Among the soldiers returning from the front maimed, with torn uniforms, sick, hungry, and out of their minds though still hanging on to a thin thread of life, we saw my father. By just looking at him as he walked in, we realized that the man who returned was different from the one who had left.

My father was changed. At the front he had caught an incurable malaria and developed heart disease, which forced him to rest all the time. All he talked about were his illnesses. He made several attempts to return to the fields and recover his former way of life, but he was so worn out that every time he tried, he would faint and we would find him, semiconscious, at some odd place. My mother therefore decided not to let him out of the house.

Though only forty years old, my father had been totally destroyed, and his condition made all of us suffer. He was always nervous, irascible, and impatient, demanding that we do nothing else but take care of him. At night fever made him delirious. Though talkative in his dreams, when awake he was very sparing with words. Each day he grew more silent, more distant; he became a stranger, not one of us. He was no longer the man who, when I was born, chose for me the name of his favorite aunt. He was no longer the man who at bedtime told me wonderful stories of princes and fairy godmothers.

The Lieutenant Major Woman

MY RELATIONSHIP WITH MY BROTHER, FRANZ, FIVE YEARS OLDER than I, grew closer after my father had become silent, but my mother continued to be my mirror and my model.

She was a beautiful lady whose main concern was to be always fair. She helped wherever help was needed, and when I had a fight with my brother, her decisions were always in favor of whoever was right. . . . She had an even prettier sister, who unfortunately died of tuberculosis at the age of twenty-two. Both sisters had ink-black, almost bluish hair. My brother and I, by contrast, were blond, like my father's family.

I think I inherited from my mother a strong sense of justice. In this connection I would like to recall an incident that has stayed with me all this time.

At Alt Moletein in those days there was a woman around fifty years old who had inherited a small farm from her parents. People called her the Lieutenant Major Woman, a nickname that so enraged her that she lost her temper whenever anybody whispered it as she walked by. Time did not forgive this woman's face, but her features, still delicate, gave evidence that in her youth she must have been a woman of great beauty. Rumors had it that she had left her parents' home at eighteen and gone to Vienna, the luxurious and bustling capital of the empire.

In Vienna she had followed the road of prostitution, associating mainly with officers of the Austrian army, and that is probably how she got her peculiar nickname. She quickly became pregnant and had a son, soon taken away from her, however, because she had contracted syphilis, then considered an incurable disease. As everybody knows, one of the symptoms of this sickness is insanity. Therefore everybody avoided her, and this wretched woman spent her days walking around town and telling stories of how all the Austrian officers, and even the emperor, had wanted to marry her.

When she walked by, kids threw stones at her and no one talked to her except my mother, who used to stop for a chat whenever they met in the street, and would give her some food and firewood. Following my mother's example, I fervently defended the Lieutenant Major Woman whenever my friends wanted to make fun of her or attack her. I felt that in this way I continued a family tradition, to defend the rights of the poor, the defenseless, the downtrodden: a heritage for which I am still grateful.

My Brother, Franz

ONE RAINY MORNING I FOUND MY BROTHER HIDING IN THE HORSE stable. He had a cigarette in his hand, and when he saw me coming in, he started to shake and mumble some words in apology. He could think of nothing better than to offer me a puff. Thus I became his accomplice and could no longer report him to our parents. I owe to Franz the discovery of a vice that I was not able to overcome until fifteen years ago.

That morning was followed by many afternoons and evenings in hiding in the granary or the horse stable to smoke. But that was not the only activity I shared with Franz. Before and after we got into smoking together secretly, we used to go into the woods a few days before the holidays, in search of a beautiful Christmas tree. When we found one, my brother would take his ax and, full of confidence, walk up to the tree and chop it down. Meanwhile, I used to wait until the pine tree was felled, watching his every move with admiration.

On one of those occasions, when I was nine, I felt too tired to keep walking and wanted to take a short nap under a tree. Franz immediately realized the danger: to fall asleep outdoors in the midst of winter, in a region where the temperature can go down to minus twenty degrees Fahrenheit, could easily mean death. Since I seemed to be in no mood to obey him, he had a bright idea. Grabbing the tree by its trunk, he had me climb onto the branches. He could then drag the pine tree with me on top. I thought this was wonderful, and we returned home laughing all the way, happy for having invented such a novel sled.

When my parents saw the pine tree along the living room floor, they gave their approval to set it up as our Christmas tree. Franz and I immediately started to trim it. On top we placed a radiant star, and on the branches small candlehold-ers with real candles. We decorated it with angels, hearts, and dolls, the meaning of which I never fully understood. But year after year we would find them in a huge box in the cellar labeled "Christmas Arrangements and Decorations." That box was the starting point for a party that seemed to have no end.

I would take care of the Advent wreath, using a piece of wood as a base and branches from the same tree to form the wreath. I would place the candles with care and devotion about two inches apart. I would decorate it with bows I made from a narrow red ribbon, and then varnish the wood to make it shine. Nothing was as beautiful as the family reunion on Christmas Eve, with all the presents under the tree. We did all the preparations and looked forward to that moment with great anticipation.

My mother's specialty was the Christmas pastry. On the table, besides the European Christmas cake made with spices, honey, molasses, and cocoa, there were chunks of cheese, jars of marmalade made at home with our own fruits, and cherry tarts.

We loved my mother's pastries and applauded gleefully when she appeared with them. Even my father, who on those occasions seemed to come out of the stupor into which he had sunk, laughed and joined us in celebrating the arrival of our favorite delicacies.

My grandmother, meanwhile, would prepare a delicious goose stuffed with apples and plums.

I loved taking part in all these preparations, because they brought our family together. We all wanted to do our share so that our Christmas would be a peaceful and happy one.

My Education

*AS SOON AS I WAS FOURTEEN, MY PARENTS SENT ME TO A RELI-*gious boarding school, where I stayed for about a year. The nuns were not particularly nice, and the food they served was so awful that it was beyond redemption.

After all these years, I still remember the smell of burnt coffee permeating the convent and my uneasiness at not getting along at all with the sisters. The fact that everybody spoke Czech was not the problem. Although it was not my mother tongue, I was able to understand it all the same. But cloistered in the convent as the sisters were, they could not understand my feelings of rebelliousness, quite natural for an adolescent who until then had been raised in the open country and without any constraints. Life at the convent was a never-ending torture for me: all we did was pray and waste time learning things that to me had no practical application whatsoever.

Years later I continued my studies in an agricultural school. I studied there for three years, a time I remember with joy because everything I was taught interested me. I was also able to make many friends, among them a Jewish girl, Rita Gross. We had a very close relationship from the moment we met.

"We don't have the same God," Rita told me one afternoon as we were leaving school.

"There is only one God, the same for everybody, Christians or Jews," I replied.

Rita looked down and remained silent for a long time while we walked home from school. Suddenly she looked straight at me with those big green eyes of hers and said, "Then why are we Jews treated as if we were inferior beings? Don't we all have a soul, and the same feelings—don't we have joys and sorrows just like everybody else? Why do people insult us and make fun of our customs? Why can't we own either a house or a piece of land?"

I did not know how to answer her, but when we said goodbye I put my hand on hers and tried to make her understand that I did not share those views and that I understood her sadness.

I loved Rita dearly; she was my best friend. Our different religions never interfered with the affection we had for each other, and our friendship lasted until the beginning of World War II. Rita was one of the many victims of Nazi savagery: she was brutally murdered by the commander of the armed forces at Alt Moletein. He was later executed by the Russians, perhaps to make us believe that eventually there is some divine justice—though it often does come too late.

My Grandmother's Laughter

IN SPITE OF MY FATHER'S ILLNESS, THE WAR, AND THE NUNS, I remember my childhood as a wonderful time. I felt protected in the bosom of my family, where there was always someone in the kitchen willing to listen over a cup of tea.

Unfortunately, that time was soon gone, never to return. Every now and then, when melancholy invades my spirits, I think of my grandmother and shudder, maybe because, like her, I am now an old woman too.

I actually remember my four grandparents very well. But, as I mentioned before, my closest relationship was with my paternal grandmother, Anna, perhaps because her home was close to ours. Our house was in the midst of a large tract of land, and she lived together with my grandfather, as well as the farm hands, at one end of the property.

She was a tall woman, slender and beautiful, and extremely bright; she knew how to take charge of people as well as situations. She had been raised in the home of an uncle elevated to the position of cardinal in a city not far from Alt Moletein. One day when my grandfather Franz was young, he went to that town in search of a sweetheart, and passing by the cardinal's house he saw Anna, then sixteen, standing by the door. He was smitten.

Grandma Anna was always a very active, lively woman who, at the age of eighty-six, still read the newspaper every day, and without the help of eyeglasses. She was stern, but I still loved her dearly. What she forbade others, she would let me do. She was always warm, open, and understanding toward me, and tolerated mischief that not even my very patient mother would let me get away with. She often took me along when she visited her friends or my uncle, who, if I had behaved, would reward me with five gold coins. This was a generous sum then because these were coins of the Austro-Hungarian Empire, from the time when the nobility were still dancing to Strauss waltzes and no one, not even the darkest pessimist, could have anticipated the Sarajevo disaster.

One day my father gave me two very beautiful goats, one black, the other white. I was so happy with these animals that I took them everywhere I went. But their behavior left much to be desired: they ate the garden flowers, the alfalfa at the horse stable, or they would stick their heads through the kitchen windows and drink water from our glasses, doing everything possible to drive my parents crazy.

All this mischief was more or less tolerated, but something happened that caused the Pelzl family members to lose their seemingly inexhaustible patience. I had the bright idea of hitching the goats to a small two-seat wagon and making them pull it as if they were little horses. I invited my grandmother for a ride around the fields in this original carriage.

Shortly after we were on our way, the goats started to run. I was unable to stop them, and, as was to be expected, the wagon finally tipped over with us in it. In consternation I saw how my grandmother hit the ground on her behind. Fortunately it had rained the day before, and the ground was soft.

For a few minutes we looked seriously into each other's eyes, and I noticed how my grandmother's cheeks turned from the pallor of fear to the deep red of intense wrath. When I saw how angry she was, I could only mutter that I was sorry. But she had landed in such a comical position, with her legs spread and her dress all in the mud that, helplessly, I started to laugh. And I could not stop. . . . My grandmother tried to reprimand me but burst into a loud and jolly laughter herself that still resonates in my ears. She was a woman of few laughs, so to me her reaction was patent and unquestionable proof of her affection for me.

I helped her up, and we went back home. My grandmother never again referred to the goats, the fall, or her muddy dress. But after that incident the animals were mysteriously given to one of our neighbors.

Good-bye to Innocence

CHILDHOOD AND OLD AGE ARE STRANGELY SIMILAR. WHEN WE are children, we look at the world with innocent eyes. When we are old, we are ready to forgive more easily and to face life with a more tolerant attitude.

Old age is a second period of innocence, now due to forgetfulness and intentional oversights. The effect is almost the same: what surrounds us is no longer terrible and at times even seems good to us, although our memories still carry the ghosts of hate and destruction. And the past is just

that: ghosts, shadows without substance or depth. Reality, concrete reality, that which keeps coming back to mind, is the cherished landscape of the world as we saw it for the first time.

Images of life in the countryside follow each other when I dream of the past: the trips with my brother to gather firewood in the forest, where we were intoxicated both by the fragrance emanating from the trees and by the few rays of light barely penetrating the darkness; our trips to search for mushrooms; our breakfasts of dark bread, butter, and chives; the early dawns so full of activity. . . .

All these idyllic landscapes, now shattered by the war, would soon start to dissipate with the arrival of the man who would tear me away from my hometown in order to share a fate of both happiness and grief.

PART TWO

Oskar Enters My Life

Electricity

IT WAS A THURSDAY IN AUTUMN. THE COUNTRYSIDE had begun to turn yellow, orange, green, and brown, and the fallen leaves covered the ground with a thick carpet that the wind swirled into different places and shapes, like an optical illusion. I was keeping my grandmother company; we were picking cherries, storing potatoes for the winter, and making plum preserves.

I was already twenty years old, and although I had my feet on the ground and was used to hard work, I was still dreaming of a first great love. And there I was, lost in my thoughts, when I saw a huge butterfly fluttering among the leaves of a lemon tree. It looked so magnificent, its colors so bright, and it flapped its wings in such an amazing way that it seemed to invite me to go out and look at it closely.

As I stepped out I noticed, a short distance from the house, two men who were eyeing me with curiosity. One was over fifty, tall and robust looking, and his companion was a slender youth with broad shoulders, blond hair, and deep blue eyes.

I greeted them, and the older man came closer

to me and explained the reason for their visit. He and his son had come from Brünn [Brno], the capital of Moravia, to try to sell us some new motors that could supply our house with electricity. They were a brand-new product of Czechoslovakia. He started to explain all about the advantages of having these generators, and how they operated. He assumed that I had no idea what he was talking about, but I had been informing myself about this invention for several months. I have always been very inquisitive and am always asking questions about everything, a vice or a virtue, depending on how you look at it. This is a habit I have kept even into my old age.

While the man was telling me things I almost knew by heart, I noticed that his son did not take his eyes off me. There was nothing special about him, with the exception of a certain aloofness and a particularly dignified stance unusual for someone his age. He seemed bored with what his father was saying, a long spiel about technology, electricity, and progress. He soon tried to engage my complicity by means of suggestive glances and half smiles.

I thought the situation was funny and could not help laughing, though I blushed and quickly covered my mouth. When the man had finished his sales pitch, I only asked him curtly to come another day to talk with my father because there was nobody else at home. I could not then imagine that, very shortly afterward, that aloof and likable youth would become my husband.

Beyond Words

ON SUBSEQUENT VISITS, OSKAR SCHINDLER REMAINED SILENT, but I always felt his deep blue eyes caressing me. It was a virile look, dark and penetrating, that I could not get out of

my mind for days. I later realized that what had fascinated
me, besides his looks, was the way he fixed his gaze upon me
and the intimation of his mysterious, undefinable nature. I
was also impressed by his discreet and never fully explicit
way of speaking, with the promise of a deeper meaning
beyond words being held back.

At first I had rejected him, though, not wanting anything
to do with him. But with the excuse of promoting the electric generators, his visits became more and more frequent,
until I could no longer resist. One day he stayed late at the
farm, and when the blue September moon rose over the
plum trees, he kissed me for the first time.

Although I did not completely trust Oskar, his passionate
kisses and embraces swept away all my doubts. After some
time, his mother and sister visited us. One evening he asked
to speak to my parents because, as he said, he had "something important to tell them." Taking me by the hand, and
fixing his beautiful blue eyes on my parents, he addressed
first my father and then my mother, and in a deep voice
made a statement I shall never forget, because it was later
proven to be both quite truthful and totally impractical.

"I want to unite my life to Emilie's, so that we can build a
future together."

At the same time Oskar was asking for my hand, I began
to analyze my situation: my father was always sick and bad
tempered, my grandmother was suffering from the ailments
of old age, and my mother, overwhelmed by taking care of
them and keeping house, had no time even to talk with her
children. Besides, my brother was becoming more and more
independent from our family life. In view of these circumstances, Oskar's proposal to share his life with me sounded
almost irresistible.

It was then, in fact, not a very difficult decision at all. I
think that today I would act very differently, but at twenty I

was ready to believe everything my heart was telling me: the words fully expressed and the others that were not, the special light in his eyes and the promised warmth that seemed to emanate from him, my emotional response to his kisses and caresses, the protectiveness of his broad shoulders, and his passionate being.

We were married a short time afterward. The wedding celebration took place on March 6, 1928, in an inn on the outskirts of Zwittau, Oskar's hometown and where he was still living with his family. There were many guests and no shortage of food or wine. While I was dancing in my short white wedding dress, my grandmother did not tire of telling everybody that in that dress I looked like Sleeping Beauty, just awakened from her long sleep by a handsome prince.

We went to live in Zwittau, then an important industrial city. We moved in with my in-laws on Iglau Street, in the family house that Oskar's mother had bought long before. They stayed on the ground floor, while we settled on the floor above.

I was never happy there, because of my very frequent disagreements with Oskar's father. My mother-in-law was practically confined to her bed, and I remember one occasion when I was keeping her company, with my sheepdog lying at my feet. Suddenly my father-in-law stumbled into the house, totally drunk, carrying in one hand a cake and with the other holding on to any support he could find along his way. He noticed my look of disapproval—for that he was sober enough—and when he was about to say something to me, I cut him off. He was furious, and since he could not throw me out, he kicked my dog out of the house while repeating over and over, in his drunken babble, that animals belonged on the street, well aware that this would annoy me no end.

Oskar's mother—whose name was Francisca Luser and whom everybody called Fanny—was an elegant and pleasant woman. She had been sick for a long time and died at fifty-three. Her husband, in contrast, was a completely uneducated man who had started off as an insurance salesman and, after going bankrupt, had ventured into the electric generator business. Hans Schindler was always traveling, but nobody seemed to miss him.

Oskar had a younger sister, Elfriede, thirteen at the time and a replica of her father: she was ugly, with dark hair and bulgy brown eyes, and nobody seemed to be paying much attention to her. Maybe that is why she became attached to me right away. I helped her with her homework and talked with her in the little free time I had left, as I had to take care of not only my own home but also that of my mother-in-law, who was in no condition to do any kind of housework.

The Ascetic and the Sybarite

MY FIRST TRIP TO PRAGUE, IN THE FALL OF 1928, WAS TO arrange for some documents Oskar needed. I was fascinated by everything: the church steeples rising proudly like needles painted on the blue sky, the stores, the streets full of people, the evenings when the city was fully lit up and reflected in the peaceful waters of the Moldau River. . . .

Prague, however, marked the end of the romantic period in my life. Imperceptibly, from that time on everything turned increasingly sad and somber. . . .

My father had given Oskar a dowry of one hundred thousand Czech crowns, a very considerable sum in those days. With that money Oskar bought a luxury car and squandered the rest on outings or unimportant things. When I protested, he replied, "Emilie, you are too austere, a real ascetic. While, on the other hand, I am by nature a sybarite!"

For months I struggled trying to understand his attitude

and concluded that it was the result of his upbringing. His mother had pampered him, and his father, busy with his so-called business deals, was seldom home.

In spite of his flaws, Oskar had a big heart and was always ready to help whoever was in need. He was affable, kind, extremely generous and charitable, but at the same time, not mature at all. He constantly lied and deceived me, and later returned feeling sorry, like a boy caught in mischief, asking to be forgiven one more time. . . . And then we would start all over again.

My days in Zwittau were spent cooking, sewing, knitting, and listening to my mother-in-law, who never stopped repeating, "Oskar is now married, and it is his wife's obligation to educate him, my dear Emilie."

She would throw these words into the air and then stare into space motionless for a long time. Resigned, I kept silent.

A short time later, fortunately, we moved into a huge house that had belonged to a wealthy Zwittau family. The mansion was full of luxurious carpets, beautiful furniture, all lit in the evenings by crystal chandeliers. The place itself was the symbol of a time of splendor that was soon to disappear.

With Me or Against Me?

WHILE MY MARRIED LIFE ALTERNATED BETWEEN GRIEF AND happiness, the affairs of the world were deteriorating: Adolf Hitler had risen to power in Germany. I shudder just at the mention of his name, the absolute symbol of cruelty and destruction, of hatred and human misery.

Who was this man who, in spite of his shadowy past, rose suddenly to power and was deemed the savior of a country torn by the most terrible social, political, and economic crisis in its history? What was in the hearts of those who considered him their leader, who would blindly follow him anywhere and surround him with adulation? What was happening to us Germans?

Of course, not every German was a Nazi. I know because I lived within that hell. But the pressure to conform was intense, and very few dared to be themselves. Hitler had been very clear: "Whoever is with me will be able to live in a great Germany. But whoever is against me will find instant death. For those, there will be no reprieve; there will be only winners. And we will be the winners. Germany, Germany, above everything, today you are ours, and tomorrow the world will be ours."

Hitler's rise marked the beginning of an indescribable tragedy: *Kristallnacht*, the concentration camps, the Nuremberg laws that forbade Jews to practice their professions, the death of millions and millions of human beings. . . .

Dragged along by the circumstances, Oskar and I became, to some extent, accomplices to what was going on. It is true that today I am proud of having worked together with my husband in the rescue of thirteen hundred Jews, but it fills me with anguish to think how small that number is compared with the number of victims who were sacrificed in the Nazi Holocaust.

I cannot but ask myself whether human beings shall one day understand that the only solution for mankind is peace. However, whenever I read or listen to someone speak about the many interests that are at play when there is a war, I realize that my ideas are pretty naive.

Spies for the Third Reich

IN 1935 OSKAR VISITED CRACOW, WHERE HE MET A WOMAN with whom he began a conversation that probably, as was his habit, ended up in some secluded place. That woman worked for the German Counterintelligence Service (Abwehrdienst), and she got him a recommendation with her superiors. Oskar really liked this new job, which consisted of locating and persecuting foreign spies in Poland.

The chief of the Counterintelligence Service, headquartered in Berlin, was Commander Hartmut, while Major von Kohrab was in charge of the Polish section. Von Kohrab belonged to the Hungarian nobility, but he had a dark secret: he was the son of a Jewish woman.

Von Kohrab managed to keep his secret for quite some time, until one of his nephews, perhaps more out of stupidity than malice, reported the major's Jewish origin in connection with some bureaucratic procedure. The counterintelligence chief in Poland had to pay dearly for this: he lost his rank and honors and then disappeared completely, without our ever hearing another word concerning his fate. I still remember him, blond and Apollonian in his elegant uniform: a man who, despite his Jewish origin, physically represented better than most, including the Führer himself, the paragons of race and beauty that Nazism was championing.

After some time the Counterintelligence Service decided to send Oskar to Mährisch Ostrau, the capital of Moldavia, to be in charge of the local section.

We had to abandon the huge house into which we had moved after living with Oskar's parents for a few years. It was very difficult to take our belongings with us. Everything was meticulously and carefully controlled: packed, loaded onto a moving van, and taken to our new home, some two hundred and fifty miles from Zwittau.

The apartment that the Counterintelligence Service had assigned to us was located at 24 Parkstrasse, right in the center of Mährisch Ostrau, facing the German army barracks, from which soldiers were continually being dispatched to patrol the streets. We had two large rooms with windows overlooking the garden. The kitchen was very comfortable, and in time it turned out to be the coziest place in the house. One of the rooms became our bedroom, while the other was made into an office.

I tried to help Oskar in his counterintelligence work. I would answer the telephone, receive messages, run errands, and type, while at the same time taking care of my domestic chores. The Parkstrasse apartment became our headquarters. There we received, processed, and concealed information, making sure it was out of the reach of any other foreign agent. In one corner of the closet we kept a Luger pistol, German army issue, always loaded. . . .

We had four co-workers, one of them a woman of Czech origin with whom Oskar also had an affair, in his now seemingly inevitable pattern. \\

One afternoon, on my return from a trip, I found our apartment in shambles: clothes out of their drawers, papers strewn all over the floor, broken lamps, a truly devastating sight. The only sound to be heard was that of the telephone, off the hook and thrown on the floor, under a layer of clothes, torn papers, busted pillows and feathers, shards from porcelain vases and dishes that apparently had been thrown furiously against the walls by our desperate visitors, frustrated because they did not find any of the things they supposedly had come for.

Nothing important had been stolen. The only thing missing was a watch my mother had given me, and which I later discovered in a pawnshop.

The second episode linked to Oskar's counterintelligence work could have ended tragically. One night, after one of our many quarrels about his extramarital affairs, I was sleeping on a couch in the office while he slept in the bedroom. Suddenly there was a noise by the window.

Ever since Oskar started in this job I found it difficult to fall asleep, and then, even in my sleep, I remained in a near-alert state. I could not get used to this almost wartime lifestyle and felt completely overwhelmed with anxiety.

The noise at the window was followed by the sound of footsteps, and a beam of light, probably from a flashlight, lit up my face for a few seconds. I got up right away and, as silently as possible, went into the bedroom, where Oskar was sleeping peacefully in our large bed. I looked for the Luger in the dark closet, walked up to the window, drew open the heavy curtain, and fired two shots in the air. I saw a shadow running, as if disoriented, toward the barracks. Apparently the soldier on duty had fallen asleep. The shadow ran well past the checkpoint and disappeared into the darkness of night.

Days later we found out that the men trying to break into our house in search of information were Polish agents.

The following is an example of the activities we had gotten involved in. A Polish soldier was paid to get us a Polish army uniform. It was then sent to Germany to serve as a pattern for manufacturing more Polish uniforms that spies of the Third Reich would wear as camouflage. When Germany invaded Poland, the SS were wearing these uniforms in the attack on the Cracow radio station but then blamed the Polish resistance for acts of sabotage.

Our Parkstrasse apartment became the permanent meeting place for spies and informers. One day the police came and started to turn the apartment upside down, looking for certain documents that Oskar had hidden behind a bedroom mirror. They finally found them, and Oskar was arrested. He had been betrayed by a Czech agent who pretended to be his friend.

Oskar was condemned to death for his offense. The German invasion of Czechoslovakia in 1939 saved his life.

Death and Its Omens

THE YEAR 1939 WAS A SAD ONE FOR ME.

First my mother died. On the very day of her death, I had been nervous and short-tempered, as if sensing that something terrible was about to happen. When I fell asleep on an armchair in our Mährisch Ostrau home, I had a nightmare: I was in the countryside, and my mother passed by in a carriage on her way to heaven. She was greeting me, waving at me through a darkish window. I signaled her to stop and begged her to stay, but the carriage kept moving farther and farther away from me.

I don't know how long the dream lasted; to me it seemed an eternity. When I woke up, I was soaked in sweat, my head seemed to be floating in a nebula, and the veins in my temples were throbbing as if all of my blood had been summoned there. I went into the kitchen and had a glass of milk, trying to calm down. On the following morning when I told Oskar about my nightmare, he looked at me in disbelief. "You give dreams too much importance, Emilie," he said. "It's impossible to predict the future."

"You see only what is expedient for you," I replied. "It is time for you to pay attention to what is happening to us, to think of us. You treat me as if I were one of those women who mindlessly always do what you tell them. I am not one of them, Oskar, and you should have realized that by now."

I noticed at once that my response had nothing to do with his comment but with the certain, terrible implications of my dream. My distress was such that I could not bear his contradicting me. When he tried to end the discussion with an embrace, I slipped out of his arms and locked myself in the bedroom to cry. It took me a while to calm down. However, I was trying desperately to let his words convince me, doing my best to exorcise my somber foreboding, to dissolve the powerful influence that the images of my dream were exercising on me.

When the telegram arrived informing me of the death of my mother, I was not surprised. It was as if my dream had been our last good-bye. My sorrow slowly gave way to other emotions. A feeling of utter despair came over me: I had been a daughter all my life, and suddenly I was alone and felt I had lost forever the protection and care that only a mother can provide.

And that's the way she died, a mother until the end. She managed to leave food for the evening, knowing that no one would cook in her place. Then she fainted, and doctors could do nothing to revive her. She was gone forever, but the table was served: there were dishes with meat, potatoes, and even dessert for those of us left behind.

My father followed her four months later. Gone was my mother's loving care to ensure that he took his medications and had his hot-water bottle at bedtime. He was still so weakened from the malaria he caught during the war that by now he could not handle the bouts by himself. When I heard of his death, the pain was perhaps less intense because ever since he had been so sick it was to be expected. Spiritually we had already come to terms with it.

My father really died of sadness and loneliness. He gave

up and just waited for the end. A few months after my mother's death, I suddenly felt the urgent need to go to Alt Moletein to see my father. I asked Viktorka, our maid and cook, to call a taxi to get me to the train station as quickly as possible. When I arrived at my hometown, my brother was already waiting for me. His telegram with the sad news had not reached me. On March 14, 1939, following an ultimatum, Emil Hácha, president of Czechoslovakia, signed in Berlin our country's surrender to the Third Reich. Two days later troops occupied all the lands of the new German protectorate. From the windows of my home I could see the large infantry contingents with their icy stares beneath their helmets, displaying their guns and marching through the streets like Roman legions. The tanks and the heavy artillery came after them, blanketing the streets of the peaceful city with a deafening clatter.

The columns of troops seemed endless, and in their midst, in an open convertible, was the man who would be responsible for the greatest catastrophe in the history of humanity. Proud like all who perceive themselves as conquerors, Hitler sat very straight. His eyes resembled two circles of fire, and his look seemed to penetrate and leave an indelible mark on people.

A Bit of History

HERE ARE A FEW FACTS THAT PERHAPS MAY GIVE A BETTER understanding of the invasion of Czechoslovakia. Many of these details I learned only later, when I found time to read books about history but without having to suffer it in the flesh.

In 1919, by the Treaty of Saint Germain signed in Paris, the Austro-Hungarian Empire was broken up forever, its

huge territory divided into a number of free states. One of
these, Czechoslovakia, was authorized by those who won
World War I (France, England, Italy, and the United States)
to establish itself as a republic in the territories of Slovakia
(until then known as High Hungary) and the Sudetenland.
Its 1939 population was fourteen and a half million people,
of whom seven million were Czechs, a little over two million
Slovaks, three million Germans, and the rest a mix of
Hungarians, Ukrainians, and Poles. The Germans lived
mainly in the mountainous regions and in the large cities:
Carlsbad, Marienbad, Franzensbad, and Heissequellen.

Our homeland was then known as Bohemia, the Latin
name of the area occupied by the Boii, a Celtic tribe who
came from Moravia. Among Germans, Bohemia was known
as the Sudeten. This name refers to the Sudety Mountains,
which extend for approximately two hundred miles.

The year 1938 marked the beginning of the German protectorate of Moravia and Bohemia, a situation that remained
in effect until the end of the war. The German policy for the
region combined brutality with demagoguery. While the
workers received extra food rations, the politicians, scien-
tists, artists, and writers were persecuted without respite.
The purpose of the invaders was to quickly transform the
region into an economic paradise and to extract the greatest
possible gain from its industrial development. The Nazis
intended to make the country into a purely Aryan territory,
where those who were "racially adequate" would be
Germanized, while the rest of the population would be
deported to various destinations. The persecution of the
hundred thousand Jews who lived in the protectorate began
in 1942. About two-thirds of them died in concentration
camps, together with some thirty-eight thousand non-Jews.

As soon as the German protectorate was created,
President Eduard Beneš formed a government in exile to

combat the invading forces. In 1939 the collaborationist regime of Emil Hácha signed the surrender to the Third Reich, in the midst of general indifference among Western nations unable to perceive the danger to the world of Hitler's increasing power.

In 1933 the Patriotic Front of Sudeten Germans was formed, under the leadership of Konrad Henlein, a man who favored National Socialist principles. Two years later, it was the second-most-important party in Czechoslovakia. One of Henlein's first moves was to request the annexation of the Sudetenland to the Third Reich. This position served him well: in 1938 he was appointed head of the German commissariat in Bohemia and Moravia, and the following year he was honored with the position of *Gauleiter*, a word coined by the Nazis to designate their deputies in occupied territories.

For the most part, the Patriotic Front was made up of workers. Oskar joined, paid the initiation fees, and received his badge. Within a few months, however, he tired of having to go to meetings and listen to speeches, so he gradually stopped attending and paying his dues. Oskar was not a man of political principles: he just acted according to the circumstances.

The enthusiasm of Henlein's followers diminished as the pressures from Berlin increased. The influence of the central government was ever more evident: the Hitler Youth was created, and the currency was devalued until it was definitively replaced by the reichsmark. We Germans of the Sudetenland were starting to lose our freedom and to feel like foreigners in our own land.

The Persecutions

AT THE BEGINNING OF THE OCCUPATION, THE SITUATION OF THE
Jews in Czechoslovakia was tolerable. The persecutions
started in 1942, after the attempt on the life of Reinhard
Heydrich, Henlein's successor. Heydrich had started his
administration with a provocation to the Czech people. In
his first speech he dared say that "the Czechs, especially
those of Bohemia and Moravia, have lost nothing with the
invasion," after which he ordered the arrest of some five
thousand people, four hundred of whom were summarily
executed.

As a logical consequence, two officers of the army in
exile, a Slovak and a Czech, mounted an attempt on
Heydrich's life, which he, after suffering an agony that lasted
over a week, did not survive. The Nazi government's retalia-
tion was cruel and absolutely disproportionate to the act.
The cars on one train were marked with the acronym "AaH"
(Attentat auf Heydrich) when it left Prague with a thousand
Jews headed for an extermination camp in Poland, followed
by the transfer from Theresienstadt of another three thousand Jews. Next, attention was directed to the town of
Lidice, near Prague. On the night of June 9, 1942, after surrounding the town, a commando unit executed some two
hundred men, while another two hundred women and children were deported to a concentration camp, of whom only
sixteen children survived. Shortly afterward, it became
known that no one in Lidice had been aware of or had anything to do with the attempt. But this was too late for the
revenge-thirsty Nazis, for whom death was part of a day's
work, as evidenced by the incessant repetition of acts of this
nature, especially against Jews.

In those days I developed a kidney problem and put myself in the hands of a female German physician of Jewish ancestry who had come from Berlin. During one of my visits, after we had become well acquainted, she told me that she had been forced to leave her native city with her mother in 1939 because the situation of the Jews had become very threatening. While she spoke, I noticed a growing sadness in her eyes that gave way to an expression of profound sorrow. Though she tried to conceal her emotion, grief seemed to overcome her and sap all of her strength.

By stages, I slowly recovered, so my visits to the doctor's office became less frequent. On my last visit for a final checkup two months later, she was no longer there. After some investigating I was able to find out that, together with her mother, she had emigrated to Africa. The word "emigrated" was deceptive: in reality she had escaped to save her life.

PART THREE

Schindler's List

Occupied Poland

IN THE MIDDLE OF SEPTEMBER 1939 HITLER INVAD-
ed Poland.

Patriotic forces were able to resist for only eight days the implacable power of the Wehrmacht.

A month later, Oskar traveled to Cracow, seat of the Governor General of the Third Reich in Poland, to receive orders from the Counterintelligence Service. In November he settled permanently in Cracow. I visited him frequently, almost twice weekly. I used to leave Viktorka, my housekeeper, in charge of the house and take a train that, following the course of the Vistula, left me at the huge train station in Cracow, capital of the earldom of Woiwodschaft.

Every time I got off the train, I discovered something new: the ancient university walls, the huge windows of Wawel, the Gothic palace from which the German command ruled the destinies of the Polish people. Not far from the station, at Pomorka Street, was the SS headquarters, the building most feared by the inhabitants of a city that, invaded on many occasions during its long history, this time experienced terror as never before.

Zwittau:
the city where Oskar
and I settled after our
marriage.

Oskar began deepening his relationship with high Nazi officials, and shortly thereafter he was offered the administration of an enamelware factory that had been owned by a group of Jewish industrialists. The plant was located at Lipowa Street and renamed Deutsche Emailwaren Fabrik (German Enamelware Factory), also known as DEF.

Oskar's expansive personality helped to simplify matters even in the most difficult of circumstances. As soon as he began talking, everybody would listen, and he was able to convince everyone with his brilliant eloquence. He made himself look important in other people's eyes just through his conviction of his own importance. It was therefore not difficult for him to establish relationships with the right people when circumstances demanded. I was more apprehensive and tried often to warn him, "Be more careful, Oskar. These times call for more caution. . . ."

He would look at me as if heeding my words, but he continued to follow his own judgment.

The more I listened to what the Nazi leaders were saying, the less I could assuage my intense fear. I was terrified by their constant declarations about the glorious destiny of Germany and their determination to impose National Socialism by force of arms and ruthless domination. I sensed that those words anticipated misfortune for the world, as well as for us, even though in their eyes we had all the advantages. But my protests to Oskar, repeated over and over again, were of no use. By the time he realized what was happening, the war had already claimed most of its victims.

Every time I returned to Mährisch Ostrau from Cracow, brooding over my disagreements with Oskar and my mistrust of the purposes of Nazism, I was faced with the placid, unperturbed gaze of my housekeeper, Viktorka, totally oblivious to everything that was going on, and with the uneasy feeling provoked in me by the two guards assigned to our home since the burglary attempt. These Czech guards, once they had eaten their fill, used to fall fast asleep on the big armchairs in our living room. They seemed to be the ones in need of protection.

In spite of all this, life in general seemed pretty normal and uneventful. Oskar was busy with his counterintelligence work in Cracow, and I tried to adjust to life in Mährisch Ostrau. I lived in a very centrally located row house, only a few minutes away from the liveliest part of town and from the city's main stores, where I did my shopping.

The Cook and the Officer

I WAS THEN A PERSISTENT YOUNG WOMAN. I LIKED TO COMPARE prices and check the quality of the goods I purchased, and would argue tirelessly with the merchants until I got what I wanted.

Viktorka lived with us. She was an excellent cook and kept a clean and orderly house. She had a good heart but was rather stubborn. Her hair, although she was over fifty, was dyed bright red and always nicely groomed. On her day off she used to dress in her finest clothes and wear a green felt hat with a small, thin feather on the side, Tyrolean style, and a black leather handbag. Then she would walk to the most popular café in town and order black coffee and a piece of hot apple tart with lots of whipped cream and cinnamon. Viktorka could have spent the rest of her life sitting in a café. This was her favorite place in the world.

One evening, after I had returned from doing my shopping, Viktorka came to me to find out which stemware to set at the table that evening. I then remembered we were expecting a visitor at eight. I told her to set our best, the red Baccarat glasses for the red wine, the green Baccarat for the white.

I was in a very good mood that evening because Oskar had sent me a bunch of beautiful red roses. I busied myself around the house, singing one of the popular songs at the time, which went like this:

> *Two red roses and a passionate kiss:*
> *There's no better way to greet a woman.*

At eight o'clock sharp the bell rang. Our visitor showed up in an impeccable German army uniform, with enough braids and medals to indicate his high position. He slowly removed his gloves, cap, and coat. I ushered him into the living room, where he sat down on a large green velvet armchair. Oskar arrived almost immediately and greeted the German officer very cordially, as if they were old comrades. The conversation began to turn political. I interjected a comment here and there so that they would not notice my absolute lack of interest in the topic of their conversation.

During dinner Oskar and the German officer continued drinking. Their conversation involved political dignitaries of ever greater importance. Suddenly the officer stood up to propose a toast and shouted "Long live the Führer! Long live the Führer!" while hurling my beautiful Baccarat glass against the piano in the corner of the dining room.

I was overcome by such hatred and fury that I lost control and told him, in a strong, steady voice:

"You can wish the Führer a long life if you like . . . but I will not allow you to break my Baccarat glasses, which were a gift from my mother. If you do it again, I will find it necessary to ask you to leave and never ever come back."

This was my first act of rebellion against a representative of the Third Reich.

Pigeons Set Free

OSKAR'S COUNTERINTELLIGENCE WORK INVOLVED OTHER types of domestic burdens for me. In the belief that they might be useful for sending information, he brought home three large cages with some forty carrier pigeons, installing them in a shed on the terrace. As was to be expected, to my many existing duties a few more were added: feeding the pigeons, keeping the shed clean, and changing their water every day.

The poor pigeons never got to serve the Third Reich, because Oskar quickly lost interest in them, as happened with most everything, once he had it. After a couple of months, tired of the unpleasant job of cleaning their droppings, I decided to open their cages. It was a beautiful sight. The pigeons fluttered anxiously by the door trying to get out, and then, after a long reconnaissance flight over the house, which I took as a good-bye, they disappeared over the horizon. I later found out that they had returned to Mährisch Ostrau, from where we heard the complaint that we had not taken good care of them.

Rumors about Auschwitz

IN 1941, AFTER A SMALL PARTY TO CELEBRATE OSKAR'S THIRTY-fourth birthday, we finally moved to Cracow. Since it has always been easy for me to learn languages, I was soon able to speak Polish well enough to make myself understood with relative ease. It also helped that as a child I had learned some Polish from my father, who was perfectly fluent. It was different for Oskar, who often had to ask me for help when talking with the locals.

Cracow lies about thirty miles from Auschwitz. Perhaps its proximity to that monstrous place, which conveys a sense of shame to so many people, explains why this beautiful city is currently not included in the tours offered to visitors by the Polish authorities. But to ignore Auschwitz is not the best way to prevent a future recurrence of the horrendous events associated with it.

History is undeniably there, and one can find enough of it by walking along the streets of Cracow. Just to visit Wawelberg Castle, residence of Hans Frank, governor-general of the Third Reich from 1939 to 1945, is to learn about the insanity that drove this man to intend to dynamite the city at the end of the war, a catastrophe fortunately prevented by the arrival of the Russian forces.

Cracow had known better times when Kazimierz still existed, the Jewish quarter that had become a financial and cultural center. The Gothic cathedral is over seven centuries old. It is a beautiful building, with its prominent display, designed by the German sculptor Veit Stoss, of King Casimir Jagiello's marble tomb. Oskar fell in love with the bustling life and beauty of the city and did not want to leave; he was more faithful to it than to many of his women, certainly more so than to me.

We lived in an apartment that Oskar had purchased from a very wealthy Jewish family. The luxury was evident in the porcelain vases, Persian rugs, tapestries, and heavy velvet curtains. The windows opened on the Planty, a group of parks that followed the contours of the old city walls near the Wawel fortress.

Before I finally moved to Cracow, Oskar used to take his lovers to the apartment, especially two of them: the one mentioned in Keneally's book as "Ingrid" but whose real name is Amelia, and a Polish woman, Viktoria Klonowska. Amelia worked with him in counterintelligence, while

Viktoria, thanks to her contacts with high authorities, improved Oskar's connections with the Gestapo.

Loneliness and Hospitals

BEFORE I MOVED IN WITH OSKAR AGAIN, I HAD VISITED HIS apartment many times. Whenever I arrived, his lovers would vanish into thin air, although Oskar did not manage to conceal entirely what was going on during my absence. I had realized that he was not sleeping alone, but I chose to look the other way. I knew much more than he imagined, and even got to know some of his women personally.

My back problems had started some time before. I had a bad fall and fractured a vertebra, which every now and then caused me such intense pain that I had to stay in bed for days at a time. I could not walk, and the ailment was immobilizing me more and more. The trip from Mährisch Ostrau to Alt Moletein to visit my parents became an ordeal. I had to make a transfer at Olmütz, and then the train went through Hohenstadt and Brerau, stopping for almost an hour. When I arrived at my destination, I was literally a physical wreck.

I had been to several Polish specialists, but none of them could put an end to my agony. Thanks to Oskar's contacts, I was able to obtain a permit for treatment at the Auguste Hospital in Berlin, accessible only to the aristocracy and to high-ranking officers of the German army.

I began my journey to Berlin on a gray and windy morning. I felt very unhappy about having to leave Oskar alone in Cracow, but the pain was becoming increasingly unbearable. The train started to pull away slowly, while my husband at the station waved a white handkerchief and got smaller and smaller. I could not stop thinking during my entire trip of

what he would be doing in my absence, that is, of all his likely infidelities.

Berlin fascinated me from the very beginning. First, the
Brandenburg Gate with its magnificent Roman chariot; to its
right, the Reichstag, with its huge proclamation on the
facade, "To the German People"; and then all the places that
had made Berlin famous: the zoo, Unter den Linden Avenue,
the cathedral, the small bridges over the Spree River,
Museum Island. . . .

Once at the hospital, I was received and taken care of
with complete dedication and kindness. My doctor,
Professor Kurt Enger, was the director of the hospital. He
was a serious man who spoke little, but as I got to know him
better, I found him to be a compassionate man who always
treated me as if I were his daughter. He was around sixty and
had acquired extensive experience in ailments like mine.
After ordering a series of X rays, he extracted a marrow sam-
ple to better analyze the possible cause of my pain. The diag-
nosis did not take long. I was never a crybaby, but when I
was informed of the seriousness of my condition, I could not
help breaking down in tears.

I spent a total of eighteen weeks in the hospital. Professor
Enger visited me twice a day, and we talked about different
subjects. When time allowed, he would invite me for a cup
of tea at his office. I can still remember him as a thickset
man in his ample white doctor's coat, making the rounds
through the hallways of the huge hospital, stopping to talk to
all his patients and inquire about their condition and their
progress, and to offer a few words of encouragement. He
was able to help me and get me out of my most difficult
moments, not just as a doctor but also as a human being. He
was my support during those difficult days I was away from
my husband, waiting for a visit that never came.

After my discharge I had to complete my recovery in

another clinic, in Austria, and a nurse from the Berlin Red Cross escorted me. She was a rough, uneducated woman who treated me as if we were in the military, forcing me to take long walks around the sanatorium and to follow an unnecessarily strict diet. Under her thumb I experienced more suffering than relief.

Finally the day came to return to Cracow. Oskar was waiting for me at the station with an enormous bouquet of flowers that I would much rather have received from his own hands at the hospital. I took them without a word, but disillusion was written all over my face. He knew me well and tried to apologize, inventing excuses to justify why he had not gone to Berlin. And, as usual, I forgave him.

Once we were home, over a glass of cognac—and for myself, a cup of tea—Oskar brought me up-to-date on what had happened during my long absence. He had made many friends in Poland, special laws had been enacted, and it was now illegal, among many other things, to travel on the express train.

At no time did he show any concern about my health. For the first time, I was scared. I felt that he no longer loved me.

Bombs on Mährisch Ostrau

ON MY RETURN TO CRACOW I BECAME CONSCIOUS THAT THE war had really started and that there would be no quick or easy end to it.

In two months I was to return to Berlin to resume my treatment. I had obtained the necessary documents and authorization for the trip and was to leave on a Friday morning. While I was packing, an inner voice kept telling me: "No, Emilie, you shouldn't go to Berlin. Do not go, do not go." Overcome by intense anguish, I could not sleep at all that night. By the time I got out of bed, I had decided to postpone my trip and stay in Cracow. A few days later, I learned that in a bombing raid the Auguste Hospital had been completely destroyed.

Some time later, however, I was to find out for myself what a bombing raid was like. In 1943, during a visit to an old friend in Mährisch Ostrau, we had just finished our coffee when I looked at my watch and realized it was time to leave if I did not want to miss my train to Cracow. I said good-bye, with the promise to return as soon as I could.

When I stepped out on the street, it was still daylight. My train was scheduled to leave in an hour, so I had time to do a little shopping. There was an awesome silence around town that puzzled me. Suddenly, high above, I heard the drone of fighter-bomber turbines. The plane had materialized out of nowhere and was maneuvering overhead as if on a reconnaissance flight. It was immediately followed by another plane, and then another. . . . Everything went silent again, and I felt a deep relief. But that calm lasted only a few seconds, and in a moment there was a deafening roar.

Bombs started dropping. There wasn't much time to get to the nearest shelter, which was about sixty yards away. While I ran I heard another explosion; I looked back quickly and saw the huge wall close to where I had been standing burst into the air in a million pieces. It had been hit by a bomb. This wall, which had witnessed hundreds of years of history, was reduced to dust in just a few seconds. War is like that: the work of a lifetime can dissolve instantly at an inconceivable speed.

In the shelter, to which people had rushed in fright, there was no empty spot. I made myself a space within that faceless mass, trying to hold my breath in the darkness. I quickly lost all sense of time. Finally someone came to report that it was all over. A desolate landscape awaited us outside.

Everything was in ruins: the streets, the houses, trees split in half. The smoke coming out of the rubble had almost made even the horizon disappear.

I later learned that U.S. fighter planes had attempted to destroy the coal deposits of the city. In less than two hours of Allied bombing, two thousand people had lost their lives on the streets of Mährish Ostrau.

War Is Good Business

EVERY EVENING SOME HIGH-RANKING OFFICER CAME VISITING to talk with Oskar. These officers differed from the SS officers, whom they despised deeply, not only in their uniforms but also in their general attitude, their education, their ideas. I tried to stay on the sidelines anyway. I did not want to listen, did not want to know. I wanted to be as far as possible from it all.

Major von Kohrab, chief of the Polish section of the Counterintelligence Service, usually stayed for dinner. Oskar had a rather close relationship with him and was perfectly aware of his secret. It was von Kohrab who, one evening during the after-dinner conversation, for the first time mentioned to my husband the possibility of his purchasing the enamelware factory. The plant, which had belonged to three Jewish industrialists of Cracow whom he knew, was in bankruptcy proceedings, and the tribunals wanted to sell it.

"It's a good business, Herr Schindler," he said with a wink.

"Yes, although a bit shady, don't you think, *Herr Kommandant?*" replied Oskar.

"In war you win and you lose, Herr Schindler," replied the officer without losing his good mood. "You buy the factory, and we'll take care of fighting the battles."

He ended up convincing my husband, who quickly arranged a meeting with the owners. Mr. Bankier, one of the three partners, visited us in January 1942, if I remember correctly. His demeanor and the way he behaved during our meeting revealed a fearful man acting as if he were living in a foreign country where he had no rights at all. He was short, round, and dark-haired. After taking off his coat and hat, he sat on the edge of the armchair, ready to leave at any moment. His expression was one of mistrust, but what impressed me most were his dark eyes, hidden behind thick glasses. They would dart back and forth quickly, as if at a single glance he had surveyed the whole place and knew exactly where everything was.

Bankier's presentation was clear. Oskar took notes and did not stop asking him questions. The price was high, but the decision to buy the factory had been made beforehand. With the agreement, not only had a contract been signed, but a pact had been entered into by people of different faiths, the consequences of which no one could then have imagined.

The Enamelware Factory

THE FACTORY WAS IN DEPLORABLE CONDITION, AND ALMOST everything had to be repaired. Oskar had to invest a great deal of money to get it going. To accomplish this he relied on the help of Isaac Stern, the factory bookkeeper, and of Mr. Bankier himself, a real wizard in the world of business.

In Spielberg's film, Stern appears to be Oskar's right-hand man. I am not sure this is exactly correct. Stern contacted me again many years after the war, five or six years after Oskar had returned to Germany. He wrote to let me know there was a contract with Metro-Goldwin-Mayer to make a movie of our story, which in the end was never filmed. I assume Oskar felt embarrassed to tell me and probably asked Stern to contact me.

The greatest difficulty in getting the factory going was obtaining the permission from the SS that would make it possible to contract Jewish workers from the Cracow ghetto, Bankier's number one condition in the sale of the plant. Once Oskar managed to obtain authorization, workers were selected according to their capabilities, health, and age. After this selection, they were all transferred to the Plaschow work camp, on the outskirts of Cracow, on lands that used to be the Jewish cemetery. The payment of wages was supposedly in the hands of the SS.

Among the Jews at the Plaschow camp, everyone who had reached fourteen years of age was obliged to work. Those under fourteen were executed or used in medical experiments. Many parents were forced to misrepresent their children's ages to save them from a certain and horrible death. Jewish women were scared of getting pregnant.

On one occasion I was approached by a young woman who told me her boyfriend had gotten her pregnant. She did not know what to do, whom to talk to, or where to go for help. I risked my life by just talking with a Jewish girl, let alone trying to do something for her. But I still felt I had to help. I talked to a doctor at a local hospital and, without mentioning that this involved a Jewish woman, asked him to take care of the problem. Even though I have always been against abortion, I thought then that there was no other possible solution.

On another occasion one of the factory workers came up to me, confused and trembling. He told me that his glasses were broken and that without them he could not work. Although each one of these requests sent shivers of fear down my spine, I always found ways to take care of them. The man finally received his new eyeglasses.

I saw these unfortunate Jewish people reduced to slavery, treated like animals, deprived of everything—including the use of underwear, regardless of the season, under their uniforms. Seeing them that way, with all their possessions and even their families taken away from them, and without the right to a dignified death, I could not but feel sorrow for their terrible fate.

Cigarettes and Bad-Tempered Dogs

AT THE CRACOW FACTORY ONE MORNING, I THREW A CIGARETTE butt on the floor. One of the Jewish workers next to me pounced on it to smoke it down to the end. An SS lieutenant who had witnessed the scene addressed me then in an angry, threatening tone:

"You discarded that butt deliberately for the Jew to have a smoke. You know very well that under no circumstances are the Jews to be favored. From now on, mind what you do, because I am going to be watching you."

"In the first place, you have no right to talk to me that way. I definitely will not allow it," I replied sharply. "In the second place, if I discarded that butt it was because it was finished. And besides, I had no intention of having anyone in particular pick it up."

Similar situations sprang up all the time. On another occasion, going for a stroll with a young Polish woman, I encountered an SS officer who was walking a small dog, almost a puppy. The animal had already passed us, when it quickly turned back and bit the girl's leg. My anger surfaced instantly, and I pulled the dog by the tail and hurled it as far away from us as I could. The SS officer made a threatening move toward me, but I confronted him, enraged:

"If you cannot control and be responsible for what your

dog does, you cannot hold me responsible for what I do. And if you take one more step, I will show you exactly who I am."

A Portrait of Amon Goeth

SHORTLY BEFORE OSKAR PURCHASED THE FACTORY, AMON Goeth, commander of the Plaschow concentration camp, was introduced to us. Goeth was the most despicable man I have ever met in my whole life. He had a double personality: on the one hand he seemed to be a refined gentleman, like a true Viennese, and on the other he seemed to relish submitting the Jews under his jurisdiction to constant terror.

To my amazement, Oskar had won his friendship and one evening brought him home for dinner. I shall never forget his physical appearance: he was more than six feet tall, had rounded, feminine hips and dark hair, and a huge mouth with fleshy lips that laughed nonstop opening as if to swallow up everything. I remember Goeth as rather slender, not as depicted in the Spielberg film, where much is made of his corpulence and weight problems.

While we talked, Goeth drank quite heavily and my husband tried to follow suit. Before his contacts with the Nazis, Oskar would have only a drop of alcohol now and then. Now he drank constantly, like his father. . . . I was afraid he would become an alcoholic.

One evening several SS officers visited us. Oskar, acting as host, would laugh obligingly while sinking into his reddish velvet armchair. Goeth was also there and, as usual, had been drinking his fill. At one point there was a knock on the door, and the servant ushered in a major of the German army. Goeth tottered up from his armchair, looked at the newcomer scornfully, and said, in a voice slurred by alcohol:

"Who are you, you ridiculous midget?"

The atmosphere became tense, and our guests began leaving one by one, offering all sorts of excuses. Goeth kept on screaming:

"You army types, you think your hands are clean. You are such aristocrats, you fight with gallantry . . . you don't stick your noses into the carrion. . . . You cowards, you claim to keep your souls clean while we have to act as your guardian angels and watch over your backs."

The fact that Oskar would spend so many hours of his life with that beast made me feel very apprehensive, because it compelled me to recognize the seriousness of the situation we were in. At Plaschow, Goeth gave free rein to his most bloody instincts. In the mornings he would get out his rifle and practice target shooting on human beings, aiming at the Jewish workers at the concentration camp. I could never understand what drove him to this, and his attitude made the human condition even more incomprehensible to me.

This man combined the most barbaric instincts with an exquisite degree of refinement. He was capable of killing in cold blood and at the same time could detect a flat note on any of the classical recordings he listened to constantly.

Edith, his lover, tried to appease him when he was in an indiscriminate killing rage, but she seldom succeeded in turning him away from this bloody practice.

It was Oskar who had introduced her to Goeth. They had a daughter, who has never admitted to her father's crimes. Edith currently lives in the United States and has tried to distance herself from this part of history. She remarried, then divorced, and now lives with another man.

In the concentration camp at Plaschow, Goeth also had a Jewish maid. He was hopelessly in love with her, and he beat her brutally every day in order to cover up his feelings for her.

This connection with Goeth caused Oskar some problems, even a few days in jail. It was not for kissing a Jewish girl, as shown in the film, but for allegedly having stored some boxes belonging to Goeth, which according to the SS contained weapons and stolen jewelry. I was present when these boxes were opened, and they contained nothing more than old clothes and uniforms not in use anymore. The only thing of value was a bag full of nuts, which were quickly gobbled up by the soldiers. One of them offered some to me, but I refused. I did not want Goeth to say I was eating his goodies without his approval.

After the war, the Czechs captured Goeth and hanged him at an army barracks. Since then, that monster appears to me in my nightmares as a terrible, bloody mask that explodes into a thousand pieces.

Nazis for Sale

THE SITUATION HAD DETERIORATED TO SUCH AN EXTENT THAT Oskar was compelled to give out ever-more-costly presents, as well as large sums of money, in order to be able to keep his Jewish workers. These "gifts" consisted of diamonds, caviar, cigarettes, cognac, and other treasures that could be obtained only on the black market at great expense.

One evening Oskar came home to our apartment in Cracow in a very depressed state of mind. With almost no word of greeting, he went straight for the cabinet in which we kept his cognac, now his constant companion.

He poured himself a goodly quantity and, without taking off his overcoat, emptied the glass in one shot, as if wanting quickly to drown a great sorrow. Being so familiar with Oskar's ways, I left him alone for a while and a little later asked him whether he was going to have any dinner. I had prepared his favorite dish, I said, cabbage and chives sautéed in butter—with the little bit of meat allowed in

1944 rations, one hundred grams [about three ounces] a day, if you were lucky. Since I never cared that much about food, I mostly left my share to him. But of course, two hundred grams of meat are greatly reduced after cooking. These portions never entirely satisfied Oskar, who was a good eater.

With an almost imperceptible gesture, he agreed to come to the table with me.

We sat down, and I served the wine and the water in a state of nervous expectation while we waited for the cook to bring the food to the table. I asked myself whether I should wait until after dinner to try to find out what was wrong. Perhaps the best thing to do, I thought, was just to bide my time, but then Oskar would most likely get up and leave the table without a word. So I took my chances.

"What is the matter, Oskar? Are we in serious trouble? What's going on?"

I assumed that his unusual grief had to do with the course the war was taking. I was not wrong.

Schindler's List

"LOOK, EMILIE," HE ANSWERED SADLY, "THE SITUATION IS becoming more and more unbearable. Goeth has decided to close the Plaschow camp and send all the prisoners, including our workers, to Auschwitz. I've talked to him several times, but I haven't been able to change his mind, no matter how hard I tried. The important thing is finding a way to move our people to some other place in order to go on working. I've been offered a munitions factory in Brünnlitz, which seems to be an ideal place. But I don't know what else to do to persuade him to authorize the transfer. I have offered him diamonds, jewelry, money, vodka, cigarettes, caviar. . . . I just can't think of anything else. Maybe I'll get him a couple of beautiful women to cheer him up, since the relationship with his latest mistress doesn't seem to be working. She is a good woman, but she keeps trying to get him off his bouts of sadism, and Goeth is getting tired of her. . . . Perhaps this will work. Another problem that worries me is the list of people we are to submit to him. I don't really know the men, their families; I barely know the names of a few who come to our office when something is needed. But I have no idea about the others. . . . I've spoken to the people who sold me the factory. One of the Jews will arrange to draw up a list of the workers we shall take to Brünnlitz. All this really worries and depresses me. I'm not used to not being in charge of things."

I listened in silence to his long and painful monologue, and for the first time he seemed to me really worried. I felt that I should help him, but did not know how, as I seldom visited the Cracow factory. Still, by the end of our conversation he seemed more relaxed, relieved. He had found someone with whom to share his worries. Even if his behavior as a husband left much to be desired, I was still his wife.

This was how the list came about. I never knew the exact name of the person who drew it up, but I think it was Goldman. A certain Dr. Schwarz from Cracow told me that he had visited this man and paid him a huge sum of money to put his wife's name on the list. When the move took place and the factory was transferred to Czechoslovakia, however, she was sent to another concentration camp, where she could have died. As fate would have it, they were reunited after the war. His wife had managed to survive almost miraculously.

Dr. Schwarz's statement, as well as stories by some others on the list, mentioning large sums of money invested to save lives, irritated both Oskar and me. My husband had not been aware of all these manipulations and frauds. It is also not true that Oskar tried to take advantage of unpaid Jewish labor. There were other similar cases, like the man who owned an army clothing factory, with three thousand Jewish workers. But one day he fled, abandoning all of his workers. The SS herded them onto an old ship and scuttled it, drowning them all.

While the war took its course and the German army was suffering setbacks at Stalingrad, Jews were being murdered in the gas chambers of extermination camps. Yet there were people who did benefit or profit from this state of affairs.

What is one person to do when every day there are dead bodies lying around everywhere, and even unidentifiable body parts of unknown victims? What should one do in the face of all those deaths, which even today haunt me in my nightmares?

That is why when someone asks me if I am pleased that the lives of so many Jewish people were saved, I answer yes, that it makes me very happy that at least there were some people who did not die in the extermination camps. It is also true, however, that at times it was very difficult to be aware of what was happening around us. Events followed one another so fast that every morning when we woke up, life seemed accidental and miraculous. It is hard to convey that feeling to those who have never experienced war.

The list included the names of the approximately three hundred Jews who worked at the enamelware factory, making cooking pots, plus those of seven hundred and fifty from the Plaschow concentration camp. As far as I could determine, the rest, to make up the thirteen hundred on the list, were those recommended by prominent people, among whom the name Goldman was later often mentioned.

Besides the approval of the list, we had to obtain a permit from the Brünnlitz quartermaster general in order to establish ourselves there. This was no easy matter, because the quartermaster general reflected the feelings of the local population, who under no circumstances wanted any Jews around. Moreover, since a munitions factory was involved, the city could become a target for Allied bombing raids, with inherent dangers to the civilian population. But it was Brünnlitz or Brünnlitz; there was no other alternative. If the permit was not granted, Oskar would be sent to the front and the Jews would be murdered, every one of them. The Plaschow camp was going to be emptied one way or the other.

I then asked Oskar to let me handle the negotiations alone. Very determined, I went to see the quartermaster general. Imagine my surprise when I was confronted by someone whose face looked more and more familiar! Little by little I realized that he was my old swimming teacher. We talked about old times, remembered old stories together, talked about his family and mine, all of which helped me with my request. I asked him for a permit, sealed and signed by him, to set up the munitions factory in Brünnlitz.

I left the quartermaster general's premises, permit in hand.

Auschwitz: Infinite Horror

THE WORKERS ARRIVED AT BRÜNNLITZ IN THE SPRING OF 1944, but the train carrying the women did not come. We all feared for their lives, even though my husband had paid Goeth a huge amount of money so that he would let the thirteen hundred people named in the famous list leave without any problems. After a couple of communications with the German command at Cracow, Oskar was able to find out that the transport with the women had been diverted to Auschwitz. Oskar was confused and nervous but, in spite of the difficulty of the situation, he decided not to be cowed and to try to do something, whatever that might be. As ever, I was ready to help him.

Oskar and I were at the office. On the table, the inevitable bottle of cognac. My husband picked up the telephone and called in Schöneborn, head engineer of the factory and part of the civilian personnel. When he came in, Oskar looked sternly into his eyes, took a small bag out of his pocket, the contents of which were very familiar to me, and addressed him in a tone of voice that did not admit any objections:

"I must entrust you with an important mission. Without the women we cannot go on with the factory. We need their labor, and besides, the men are getting very restless asking why their wives have not come yet. They fear something has gone seriously wrong. You are to go to Auschwitz immediately, speak to whomever you have to, pay whatever the price may be, but I want you to get those women here. I have full confidence in you; I know you are an honorable gentleman who can be trusted and will make good on your word."

"It will be done as you say, *Herr Direktor*," Schöneborn answered, taking the bag with the diamonds and pressing it to his chest.

He immediately asked for permission to leave, turned on his heels, and walked out. I don't doubt that Schöneborn did give the precious stones to the SS in an effort to get the women released. Time went by, and we were still without news of the Jewish female workers. Work at the factory had already started several days before, and the anxiously awaited train from Auschwitz still did not show up. We could only speculate regarding the fate of the women, and each new conjecture seemed worse than the others.

Auschwitz was, without any doubt, the most horrendous of the concentration camps created by Nazi barbarism. A perfect extermination machine where everything was meticulously planned, and where crematories and chimneys were busy day and night. Twenty-four hours of nonstop executions of people whose only sin was to profess a different religious faith.

Orders for the construction of that particular hell were given by Heinrich Himmler, head of the SS, in April of 1940. The camp was some thirty-five miles east of Cracow, and in order for it to be built, seven small Polish towns had to be evacuated. The wrought-iron lettering over the entrance gate proclaimed, "*Arbeit macht frei*" (Work makes you free). In its twenty-eight barracks, prisoners slept on straw or wooden planks, after exhausting workdays of over twelve-hour shifts. Half-starved, mistreated, and constantly beaten, those poor men and women welcomed death as a relief from such a humiliating kind of life.

In 1941 the so-called "Final Solution to the Jewish problem" was enacted, requiring an expansion of the camp as well as the construction of another one, at Birkenau, about two miles from Auschwitz. The transports would arrive at the ramps, where the prisoners were subjected to a "selection" process, carried out by the SS and the doctors who served under them. Those fit to work were segregated, the others sent directly to the gas chambers. Some were selected for "scientific" and "medical" experiments under the supervision of the sinister Dr. Joseph Mengele, known as the "Angel of Death." Children, especially twins, and disabled people of all types were sent to him.

The crematories were built in 1943, as well as the gas chambers and the ovens. From then on, the horrendous death machinery knew no rest.

On one of my many trips to take documents from Mährisch Ostrau to Cracow, I shared a train compartment with a youth and a gentleman who, seemingly frightened, kept looking nervously out the window. Observing the younger one, apparently the son, I noted that though he was probably about twenty, his poor physical condition made him look still like a boy.

He looked very sick and emaciated. His body seemed to sink into his seat, and he did not stop shivering. I asked the man whom I thought to be the father what was wrong with the boy that he looked so terribly ill. With tears in his eyes, he said that his son had been apprehended by the Gestapo in Prague and transferred to Auschwitz, where he had been subjected to medical experiments with the malaria virus. Only after many petitions, pleas, and negotiations, and in view of the boy's poor state of health, was the father finally successful in getting him released.

The boy had been accused of participating in the murder of Reinhard Heydrich, the *Gauleiter* of Bohemia and Moravia.

The Rescue of the Women: Hilde

STILL DESPAIRING ABOUT THE FATE OF THE FEMALE WORKERS, and not knowing whom else to appeal to, Oskar drove to Zwittau, where he contacted an old childhood friend, Hilde, and asked her to go to Auschwitz and personally take care of the release of the women. I do not know what contacts Hilde had with the upper echelons of the Nazi bureaucracy, but the fact is that, one way or another, she succeeded. A few days later, the train with the three hundred female prisoners arrived at the esplanade.

Hilde was the daughter of a wealthy German industrialist who one day had left for Mexico, without any luggage, and never returned. She was strikingly beautiful, slender and graceful, and her pretty blond hair drew the attention of both men and women. She followed the impulses of her independent personality and loved freedom more than anything. She never wanted to tell me why she did it, nor how she managed to attain the release of the women from the concentration camp, but I suspect her great beauty played a decisive part.

Our relationship with Hilde dated from a long time back. She belonged to our summer group and had excelled as a swimmer. Her family and Oskar's had been on very good terms. Both families were from Zwittau, a city that at the beginning of the century was small enough for everybody to know everybody else. In time I found out that Hilde worked for the Wehrmacht. Shortly after she arranged to get the women out of Auschwitz and have them sent to Brünnlitz, we lost track of Hilde. When we later looked for her, Hilde was gone, and no one could tell us what had become of her.

Nobody has spoken about Hilde, and I think that this book provides a good opportunity to offer this extraordinary woman recognition for all she did.

Rising Like the Phoenix

THE ARRIVAL AT BRÜNNLITZ OF THE TRAIN WITH THE FEMALE workers caused a great commotion. In the celebration there were tears and laughter, while the German soldiers watched in silence, their sidelong glances still threatening.

The women arrived from the concentration camp in disastrous condition—fragile, emaciated, weak. I took care myself of hand-feeding them semolina porridge and making them take their medications. They improved almost instantly, feeling protected and taken care of, safe at least as long as they stayed at Brünnlitz.

Oskar and I knew, however, that we were only a stage of the plan. One day, almost at the edge of desperation, I asked

Oskar, who was then writing a letter, "How long is all this going to last? Will this agony of war go on forever?"

"My dear Emilie," he answered with a heavy heart, looking at me with sadness in his eyes, "we have jumped into an abyss. There is no turning back."

The day we arrived at Brünnlitz, we unpacked our belongings and then took a look at the condition of the factory. The plant, formerly a spinning mill, had belonged to a Jewish businessman. It had been abandoned for some time, and everything was in disarray. There were boxes full of wool scattered in every corner, broken windows, and reminders everywhere of what once must have been a place of intense activity.

"And is it here that we're going to set up a munitions factory?" I asked my husband, desolate at the sight of the plant.

Oskar seemed calm as usual, but he answered in a voice that evidenced his concern.

"We're like the phoenix, Emilie; we'll always rise from the ashes. You'll see how quickly everything is going to change and how soon I'll have this place running."

I wanted to believe him but somehow felt that this time his words of hope had no basis whatsoever. It was like one of those other premonitions I have had from time to time.

A few days later, the blast furnace for the manufacture of ammunition was installed. It had been brought specially from Cracow. Schöneborn, who had already been the head engineer in the enamelware factory, was in charge of all these activities; he was indeed a tireless man, capable of organizing the work, repairing the machinery, and being in control of the entire production process.

*At my parents'
home, attempting
to play an old
mandolin.*

*Recently married,
while we were still
living with Oskar's
parents. Zwittau,
1929.*

Our wedding photograph. I felt like
Sleeping Beauty brought back to life by a
prince. Zwittau, 1928.

*Oskar, as elegant
as ever, during the
time he worked
for the German
Counterintelligence
Service. Mährisch
Ostrau, 1936.*

*Emilie Schindler
in Poland,
around 1940.*

LEFT. *With my dear Traude, Oskar's niece, during a winter vacation in the Sudentenland, 1941.*

BELOW. *With friends and Traude, against the snowy background of the Sudety Mountains, 1941.*

RIGHT. Traude on a huge felt bear, under the amused gaze of her aunt and a friend. Sudetenland, 1941.

BELOW. With Oskar at Mährisch Ostrau, 1942. We had just bought the enamelware factory, and we were enjoying a good moment in our relationship.

Oskar singing at a party, accompanied on the accordion by a friend, whom we met again in Munich after the war. Crakow, 1943.

Dancing at the same party. Perhaps a way to forget, even if only for a moment, the tragedy surrounding us. Crakow, 1943.

ABOVE. *Visiting Zwittau, with Elly (Oskar's sister) and Traude, 1943.*

BELOW. *A moment of happiness with Traude and my indispensable dogs. Regensburg, 1947.*

Abraham Bankier and Rega Peller Bankier, former owners of the enamelware factory at Zwittau, around 1950.

Oskar charming his female audience. On the left, his lover Gisa, who followed him to Argentina. San Vincente, 1952.

At an event of the Jewish foundation B'nai B'rith, which helped me when Oskar left permanently for Germany. Buenos Aires, 1994.

Erika Rosenberg and myself, greeting German President Roman Herzog, a very warmhearted man. Bonn, 1995.

Talking with Bill Clinton, president of the United States, at the world premiere of the film Schindler's List. *New York, 1994.*

With John Paul II, at the Vatican, 1995. An unforgettable moment.

At the entrance of the Rome synagogue, with the survivor of three concentration camps, who is showing me the numbers the Nazis branded on his arm. 1995.

At the Colosseum, during a walk in Rome, a city that received me with affection, 1995.

*This is me, Emilie. In my wrinkles
you can read, as in the lines in this
book, the story of my life.*

Working at the Plant

MISS KRONOVSKY HAD COME WITH US FROM ZWITTAU TO work at the plant. She was remarkably meticulous and punctual, and as the secretary she also had to keep up to date the lists of all those who worked at the plant. These lists had to be submitted every eight days when the food rations were delivered, supposedly calculated according to the required number of calories per person. We also received once a month a pad with vouchers for each of the workers.

Miss Kronovsky's work was strenuous and exacting because the German authorities required a lot of detailed information and did not tolerate mistakes. They inspected the books with maniacal thoroughness, and each error was punished severely and with demands of money. The supervision of the munitions plant was in the hands of the army, which had the premises enclosed with electrified wires. It posted two hundred and fifty heavily armed men under the SS *Obersturmführer* Leopold, a short, tubby Austrian, who had previously commanded a concentration camp in Budzin, Poland, where airplanes were manufactured.

As long as we were in Brünnlitz, our Jews were untouchable. But both Oskar and I were also prisoners of the Germans. If we had attempted to escape, my husband would have been sent to the front, and God knows what would have happened to me.

The general command of the area was in the charge of Officer Lange, head of all the German munitions factories. He was a gentleman, and whenever he visited us, he came dressed as a civilian, perhaps to show his disapproval of the Nazi regime. He repeatedly mentioned that he worked for his country and not for a specific government or system.

Lange was known for his rectitude and sense of justice,

and his coming to the factory did raise some fears that something might not be in line with his rigid criteria. When he
arrived from Berlin for his first inspection of the factory, I
invited him home to have lunch and to take a rest from his
long trip. Fortunately everything proceeded in the most cordial and friendly manner.

Although Brünnlitz was a little more peaceful than
Plaschow, terror was always present. Shortly after our arrival,
a woman was hanged in town, accused of having fallen in
love with an English prisoner. When the romance became
known, she was taken to headquarters and interrogated in
the most brutal manner, as if love were an unpardonable
crime. The next day she was escorted by a couple of soldiers
to a large tree in an open area and hanged. Her body was left
there in public view for eight days as an inescapable example
to all of us, to show what would happen if we helped anyone
considered to be an enemy of the Führer or the policies of
the Third Reich.

We lived in constant fear that the SS would discover that
we were helping the Jews and giving them food. Typhus was
another important enemy; since it was transmitted by lice, at
the laundry shop we boiled all clothes at two hundred forty-
eight degrees Fahrenheit to exterminate them. A plague
would have been reason enough for the Nazis to close the
Brünnlitz factory.

We had received a shipment of steel plates that were to be
tempered in our press and used in the manufacture of shells
for antitank ammunition. The plant had all essentials: tanks
of sulfuric acid, electric ovens, huge storerooms. But no
ammunition ever came out of it.

We were surrounded by high wire fences, and vigilant
guards were posted in several watchtowers. These over-
looked the river and the town, with its Skoda and Bota

manufacturing plants. In the latter, if I remember correctly, shoes were made.

We slept in a room next to a long hallway where the machinery had been set up. Our only companions were our sheepdogs, Rex and Karin. Rex was a very intelligent dog, winner of three medals because of his fine pedigree. He and Karin made a faithful couple, loyal to their owners.

The duties required by our position in Brünnlitz kept me busy all day. My job was to organize the meals of the entire factory personnel. The building had its own power, either coal burning or electric, and therefore we had both heat and hot water in winter.

In addition to the Jews on the list, a few Czechs and Poles worked at the plant. In spite of all our care and efforts, the food rations assigned by the German authorities were not always enough for everybody. The Jewish workers received larger portions because they handled the heavier work. I always tried to get them more bread than was stipulated and to make sure that the soups were as nutritious as possible. Each time they bathed, they were taken to the scales and their weight was carefully noted. The funerals, and there were not many, were held at the Catholic cemetery so that the bodies would not be burned in the factory ovens, and the gravediggers were paid with an extra two pounds of bread.

Tired of looking at weakened bodies, hungry children, and desperate mothers, I took a step that was just as necessary as it was dangerous.

An Aristocratic Lady

NOT FAR AWAY FROM OUR FACTORY THERE WAS A MILL BELONG-ing to an aristocratic lady, Frau von Daubek. I had heard she was very open and cordial, and so I decided to try my luck with her.

Shortly after having met with the manager of the mill to ask for a personal interview with the owner, I received a message from Frau von Daubek inviting me for tea at her residence the following day. I was taken aback a little by how fast things were happening, and I tried to figure out ahead of time which would be my best line of argument in order to get the mill to supply me with food for the workers. After giving the matter much thought, I decided to tell the truth: that the food I received was not enough and that I could not stand seeing our workers getting weaker by the day because of hunger.

That night I took a cup of linden tea to bed with me to try to calm myself. I was nervous and fearful. Oskar had to go to Cracow, and there was no one with whom to share my anxiety. Only the thought of the starving workers made me take the path to the mansion of the aristocratic miller lady, and as I walked, I became more and more determined not to return empty-handed. The sun was shining brightly that autumn afternoon, and I walked hugging a huge bouquet of flowers for my hostess.

Frau von Daubek was waiting for me in her enormous drawing room. In the center of the room was a round table, beautifully set, with an elegant tablecloth she had embroidered herself, she said. The tea and an array of delicacies were served in exquisite blue-and-gold Meissen china bearing the family coat of arms.

As soon as Frau von Daubek saw me come in, she rose and walked toward me with resolute steps. A little over fifty, she had a noble bearing. Her classic attire and delicate manners evidenced her aristocratic upbringing. With a slight movement of her hand, she indicated my place at the table.

"First we will serve ourselves, my dear lady, and then we will talk about what brought you here."

After we had tasted every one of the delicacies that had been served with the tea, prepared in the English manner with milk, I spoke about the purpose of my coming to visit her. I explained the situation and said that I had something to beg of her: "What I need, if possible, is grain from your mill. And it is urgent."

She asked me what reasons I had that could induce her to agree to my request. "I only want to help our Jews," I answered promptly, "and the rest of the workers, so that they will not starve to death."

The lady was listening to me attentively while folding the napkin in her hands as if this action helped her to think. After a few moments, which seemed like an eternity to me, she cleared her voice slightly and answered:

"I understand your situation perfectly and realize we are going through unfortunate and difficult times. Anyway, I would like to help if I can. Please go to the mill and speak to the manager. Tell him from me that he is to give you whatever you need for your people."

Once she had said this, she rose and very cordially said good-bye. The meeting was over, and her housekeeper came at once to show me to the door.

That afternoon I returned to the factory with a veritable treasure in grains and semolina flour.

My First Crimes

FROM ONE OF HIS MANY TRIPS TO CRACOW, OSKAR HAD brought a thousand bottles of vodka and a big box full of cig-arettes with which to bribe the SS officers. On the same evening that I met with Frau von Daubek, I waited until I could take advantage of the guard's stepping away and, with a Polish Jew named Oberek as my lookout, entered the storeroom and stole a few packs of cigarettes and a couple of bottles of vodka.

I was very much aware that if I were discovered stealing in the company of a Jew, I would be summarily executed. But it seemed that God, or good fortune, was on my side. There could be no mistakes, and I took painstaking care not to overlook even the smallest detail.

There was another Jew, Bejski, who made fake rubber stamps used on passes that allowed holders to leave the premises and go for gasoline, bread, flour, cloth, or cigarettes. Oskar had exchanged some diamonds for over two thousand pounds of bread, and I used to go back and forth to the black market negotiating and purchasing foodstuffs.

In addition to my factory duties, I had some "honorary services" to perform, such as taking care of the wives of several of the SS and army officers. So I moved from one world to the other, from the grim reality of the Jews who lived amid hunger and desperation to the world of those women whose husbands were in charge of spreading the war all over Europe.

On one occasion, a lieutenant major of the Artillery Command sent us his wife and son to get them away from the frequent bombing raids over Berlin. The three of us traveled to Mährisch Ostrau, where we still had our old apartment. Viktorka preceded us to get everything ready for our arrival.

At Mährisch Ostrau, the lieutenant major's wife and I had some disagreements. These occurred, first, because she was an alcoholic and, second, because her son, then about twelve, liked to appropriate what did not rightfully belong to him. He had taken a couple of my things: a pencil holder, a small silver vase that my mother had given me, and some other object that I have since forgotten.

This precocious thief was involved in another incident. A Polish woman who worked at the Brünnlitz factory was jailed by the SS and charged with having stolen money from the cash register. She defended her innocence so forcefully that the Germans investigated further until they decided, as was their custom, to accuse a Jewish family of the theft and execute its members summarily. Later it became known that it was the son of Commander Hartweg who had taken the money. This is the way Nazi justice worked.

These "honorary services" of mine were essential to guarantee my safety and especially that of my husband. My nerves were permanently on edge, and, in the belief that it would soothe me, I began smoking one cigarette after the other. I had no preferred brand and smoked whatever I could get. I remember there were some pretty good Polish cigarettes, but most of the others tasted like straw. Some fifteen years ago, my health forced me to stop smoking: my left foot became completely paralyzed, and there was danger that the process would continue if I did not stop. I was smoking as many as forty cigarettes a day. I did realize that it was bad for my health, but I had been unable to quit. Nothing else would calm me down.

The Jews of Goleschau

ONE NIGHT WHILE A TERRIBLE STORM WAS RAGING OUTSIDE, with the temperature dropping to twenty degrees below zero Fahrenheit and the room being frequently lit up by lightning, I heard some heavy pounding at the door. Still half asleep, I threw something over my nightgown and ran downstairs.

Oskar had not returned yet from one of his trips to Cracow, and I was alone.

At the door I asked who it was, and a masculine voice answered: "Please open up, Frau Schindler. I have to talk with you. It's important."

It was the man in charge of transporting Jewish workers from Goleschau, a Polish mine in which subhuman conditions prevailed. He was asking me to accept the two hundred and fifty Jews, crowded into four wagons, whom he had brought in. Some plant had placed a request and then rejected them when it became known that the Russian troops were approaching. If I also rejected them, they were going to be shot.

Quick action was required if I wanted to do something for them. I ran to the phone to call Oskar, explained the situation to him, and asked for permission to accept those Jews in our factory. He agreed. I hung up, got dressed, and went out to get the engineer Schöneborn. I woke him up and asked him to come with me to the huge platform serving as the train station.

It was close to daybreak and snowing heavily. We found the railroad car bolts frozen solid and tried, unsuccessfully, to pry them open with long, heavy iron bars. Schöneborn then brought a soldering iron and, with a lot of patience, finally succeeded in forcing the compartments open.

The German commander, flanked by two dogs, was watching our every move and then called me aside.

"Stay away, Frau Schindler, it's a terrible sight. You'll never be able to erase it from your mind."

I paid no attention to him and, despite his warning, walked up to the railroad cars. The spectacle I saw was a nightmare almost beyond imagination. It was impossible to distinguish the men from the women: they were all so emaciated, . . . weighing under seventy pounds most of them, they looked like skeletons. Their eyes were shining like glow-ing coals in the dark.

That image of horror and human misery comes back to me every now and then, and a feeling of helplessness grips my bones, as if I were again back at the station. Twelve of them had not survived the trip. The position of their bodies seemed to say they had spent the last moments of their lives begging for answers: hands folded and eyes wide open, as if pleading to God.

The ones who had survived needed the greatest of care. We transferred them to a sort of interim emergency hospital that was set up immediately, where they would stay for over two months. At first, they required extremely special atten-tion and even had to be spoon-fed to prevent their choking to death. After not eating for so long, they had forgotten how.

As their health improved, they started joining the work force at the plant, where they were safe and could live on the food obtained from Frau von Daubek's mill and from our black-market dealings. In the meantime, they, as well as the rest of the workers, were waiting in vain for the factory to start operating. As I mentioned before, not a single bullet ever left the plant. That factory was simply a refuge for those who had managed to evade the horrors of the concentration camps.

By then it had become evident that the end of the war was drawing near. The Russians were not far away, and rumors that they were on the brink of entering Poland were intensifying. Waiting for either salvation or death, the men spent their days tightening nuts and bolts and walking around the huge factory. The women occupied themselves knitting coats, using the wool left over from the time when the plant was a spinning mill. The atmosphere changed Friday evenings when the Kabalat Shabbat began. The anguished prayers then alternated with songs of hope.

While the Jewish workers were getting back to a way of life that, while not quite normal, at least was not so life-threatening, I kept trying to obtain food and medicines from the morning train that arrived at Mährish Ostrau invariably overflowing with Czechs, Poles, and even Germans, all of them trying to escape and not knowing where to go.

Oskar remained in Cracow, as if he could not let go of the old enamelware factory.

Viktorka

AS THE WAR WAS COMING TO AN END, I HAD A LAST MEETING with my friends at Mährisch Ostrau. The only topic of conversation was the hope that we would see each other again, once everything was over. The pervading sadness made clear that separations were inevitable.

I returned later to say good-bye to Viktorka, who had stayed in Mährisch Ostrau in charge of the house. She was standing by the window, plump and petite, with her beautifully done red hair. We looked meaningfully into each other's eyes. As if on a movie screen, memories of our times together rushed through my mind.

I remembered the fierce briskness with which she prevented everybody from entering the kitchen, her private domain, until everything was clean and shining. Once I happened to enter the kitchen at lunchtime, and I noticed that Viktorka was eating potatoes only, with none of her meat ration. I asked her why she was doing this, and for whom was she saving it? After some hesitation, she confessed she had been saving the meat for me, so that I would eat properly. At once annoyed and grateful, I ordered her to never ever do such a thing again.

As I was leaving Märisch Ostrau, I asked her why she had

her coat on. She told me that she had decided to take my train and accompany me for a while. It seemed she wanted to delay the moment of separation, to postpone it as long as possible, to make it stretch forever. . . . So we shared that last train journey to Prague. I had to get off at Böhmisch Ostrau, an important rail junction, where I would board the train back to Brünnlitz.

As soon as we sat down in our compartment, we started talking about trivial matters and things we would take up later when we met again. But that was never to occur.

At some point Viktorka interrupted our conversation to tell me that she loved me dearly, as if she were my older sister, and that she felt jealous when she saw me chatting happily with our neighbor, Frau Pirschkin. I started to laugh, though her confessions made me feel good, especially because they were about a solid and lasting affection at a time when everything around us was crumbling.

Enveloped in the evening mist, the train stopped at the Böhmisch Ostrau station, where we would say good-bye forever. As we walked arm in arm along the platform, we both knew that this would be our final farewell. I never saw Viktorka again or heard any news about her.

Waiting for the Russians

WHEN RUSSIAN AND AMERICAN TROOPS LIBERATED CZECH-oslovakia in May 1945, the sad and painful exodus of the Germans from the Sudetenland began. They were transported in cattle cars or forced to walk to the border. Sometimes they were dragged to concentration camps and required to wear identification bracelets. They were usually given just one hour to pack their belongings in one small bundle, which was all they were allowed to take. Many Czechs did not agree with these measures and tried to help their German friends at the risk of their own lives.

One afternoon Oskar turned on the radio and heard that the Russians were close to Lemper and that the situation was deteriorating by the day. Despite all evidence to the contrary, my husband firmly insisted that the Russians would never come. Dismayed, I could not believe my ears. How could such an intelligent man not realize what was going on and be so quiet and apathetic, as if he were in a daze? He seemed caught in a time warp, unable to react. It reminded me of his comments while we drove the twenty miles from Brünnlitz to Zwittau to talk with Hilde concerning the release of the Jewish women.

During the whole trip he seemed deeply worried; he said he no longer understood the meaning of that war, which had only served to kill a lot of innocent people. He kept reminiscing about the times when it was possible to live peacefully together with Jews, and he cursed the state of affairs that had led to the persecution and extermination of so many people. He seemed absolutely uninterested in anything having to do with the factory, except that thanks to its existence a few lives could be saved. Oskar had just been to Istanbul for a number of interviews with a Jewish foundation called Joint, which was determined to save as many people as possible. He also had a meeting in Budapest with a Mr. Cedlachek, who had contacted my husband through Mr. Bankier, the former owner of the Cracow factory.

As Oskar drove into the last curve before entering Zwittau, he stepped so hard on the gas, making the Horch lunge forward, that I realized he was really out of control. He was an excellent driver and knew perfectly well when to accelerate and when to slow down. But he was in a different world, far removed from what was happening around us. As usual, he had let himself be carried away by the circumstances.

Now I saw him again subject to the impulse of the moment. He was no longer the wonderfully articulate man I had known, elegantly Apollonian and capable of charming the whole world.

Germany Surrenders

ONE HOUR PAST MIDNIGHT ON MAY 9, 1945, AFTER SIX YEARS OF thundering incessantly all over Europe, guns were ordered to be silent. The war had left a balance of fifty-five million dead, thirty-five million wounded, and three million missing.

With the news that Germany had surrendered, the first to leave Brünnlitz were the SS officers. Their disbandment only confirmed a general state of mind that was clearly evident toward the end of the war. Living in a state of war for so long had brought the majority of the German people to a point of complete exhaustion. Morale had declined noticeably, and everyone was anxious for peace, no matter at what price. Little by little, Hitler, the Nazi ideals, and the crazy ambition of a thousand-year Reich had lost all meaning.

The SS had been busy eliminating the best officers of the German army, especially after the attack on the Führer's headquarters masterminded by Colonel Claus von Stauffenberg, in mid-1944. The reprisals concluded in the execution of approximately five thousand people and the arrest of the families of the officers most closely involved.

Erwin Rommel, the Desert Fox, commander of the Deutsche Afrika-Korps, was despicably murdered—contrary to the stories that circulated about his presumed suicide—for his participation in the plot against Hitler. He was kidnapped from his home, shoved into a car, driven to a solitary area, and forced to take poison.

In those days it was rumored that General Udet, the most

honored Luftwaffe pilot, had been brutally murdered for dis-
obeying orders from the high command. I also found out,
from an infantry officer of the Eighth Army returning from
Stalingrad, that the Führer had said over the radio, in view of
the imminent defeat of the Third Reich: "As long as there is
a single German left, there will be no retreat."

Those Were the Words

ON THE DAY THE ARMISTICE WAS SIGNED, OSKAR ORDERED
loudspeakers to be installed at the factory, and then he
assembled all the workers, Jews and non-Jews, in the large
central courtyard. After listening to Churchill's words
announcing the unconditional surrender of the Wehrmacht,
signed by Admiral von Friedeburg and General Jodl at
General Eisenhower's headquarters, my husband announced, standing on a high iron staircase, that in view of
the new situation the factory would close and that all of
them were free to go wherever they pleased. He also spoke
about the futility of wars and the suffering they brought to
different countries. He referred to the persecutions suffered
by the Jews, to the deaths of so many innocent people and of
so many children. He made an appeal for us all to part without rancor in our hearts and thanked the workers for their
cooperation. He advised them to find ways to rebuild their
lives as best they could, and regretted that there was nothing
more he could do for them.

Those were his words, the ones that had to be said at a
moment like this. I felt very proud to be there, at his side.

PART FOUR

After the War

Farewells

THOUSANDS AND THOUSANDS OF PEOPLE WERE
fleeing to the West, fearing the arrival of the Red
Army. Others were clamoring for their loved ones
amid the ravages of war. The survivors of concentration camps in Russia, Poland, Italy, France,
Holland, Belgium, and so many other places were
trying to find their way back to their homes.

It was the end, but also a new beginning. The
world had changed into something unrecogniz-
able. Men and women had regained their freedom, but they were still face-to-face with fear,
despair, and hunger.

That was our fate at Brünnlitz, caught between
the Russian army behind us and the Czechs
ahead. Oskar had just returned from Cracow and
seemed not to realize what was going on. Instead
of starting to move on, he was delaying the decision to leave by talking and drinking cognac with
an old childhood friend, who was later captured
by the Russians and sent to remote Siberia.

When I decided on my own to rush our departure, he walked to our bedroom and started packing slowly as if he were just getting ready for a
long pleasure trip. At the time, his attitude irritat-

ed me no end; I think today I would be more understanding.

Of course, at Brünnlitz there were no means of transportation: no trains, no trucks, no buses. And we did not have a fortune in diamonds either, as was once rumored.

I hurriedly packed all our papers and documents in a black leather handbag that I had had no chance to use until then. Tightly packed and tied with a ribbon were our documents, including birth certificates, marriage certificate, some cherished photographs of my hometown, my childhood, my parents, images that spoke of my past. There was also a genealogical family passport with the history of the entire Pelzl family. All this was to be lost as part of the vicissitudes of our flight. . . .

With quick, resolute steps we walked into the factory yard, where our Horch, a car with a strange history, awaited us. This model was even more expensive and luxurious than a Mercedes, and it had originally been made for the Shah of Persia [now Iran]. War had prevented its delivery, and since my husband was an enthusiast of fast, luxury cars, he could not resist the temptation of buying it as soon as he laid eyes on it. Its original color was sky blue, but it was later painted gray.

The reigning chaos and the fear of not being able to flee before the Russians came were such that when people saw the car, everybody wanted to get on it. But there was no space at all, it was only a two-passenger car. On the roof, or holding on to the sides of the car, about ten German soldiers managed to avoid the travails of a long march. But on reaching Deutschbrod, they had to get off because the Russian troops and the Czech civilian militia were already quartered there. All along the road, over and over again, there were the same horrible scenes of people trying to flee, surrounded by a spectacle worthy of Dante's Inferno, of German tanks scattered in the lonely fields, each exploding in the midst of a gigantic blaze.

We said good-bye to our workers, who had gathered there. All of them were visibly moved and, together with the miners from Goleschau, bade us their last farewell. I will never forget the expression on their faces, a mixture of sadness, gratitude, and hope. Nor will I ever forget their gesture of preparing a document for us, a kind of diploma, drawn on whatever pieces of paper they could find, and which most of them signed, testifying to what we had done for them. That document, however, would not have helped us much either with the Russians or with the Czechs, who were looking for Oskar because of his activities with the Counterintelligence Service.

After letting our friends know what our route would be, we got into the car, and with a small, timid gesture of good-bye, but more significant than anything we could have said, we slowly drove away. A truck with no brakes driven by Rizyard Rechen, one of our most outstanding workers, followed us at a prudent distance with seven people perched on the back. My husband's first plan was to get as far as Pilsen, but since he had forgotten to take a map, we never made it there.

We had been on the road for quite a while when all of a sudden Oskar stepped on the brakes. Frightened, I asked him what was wrong. Pointing to the glove compartment, he told me he had brought along a huge diamond, which he wanted to hide under the seat on the right side. He asked me to get out, and I obeyed without a word. I just couldn't recover from my amazement.

Without Destination

THE TRIP WAS LONG, VERY LONG. WE DROVE THROUGH TOWNS and cities, and everywhere the same scenes of desperation and of people trying to flee were repeated over and over. The desolation was overwhelming, and everything seemed destined to eternal damnation. I remember seeing on one side of the road a German general left behind by his men when their car went into a ditch, screaming for help at the top of his lungs. No one was paying any attention.

Only the trees were still standing in these razed lands, prevailing obstinately in the midst of desolation. Their branches, reaching up into the sky, seemed to be pleading together with all the men and women leaving their homes, perhaps forever. Our friends in the truck surely shared the same sadness, but they were now free at last. On the other hand, what would happen to Oskar and me if we fell into the hands of the Russians or the Czechs?

I could not help speculating on what our fate would be, while weariness was taking hold of me, making my reflections even more ominous. The following morning we arrived at Deutschbrod, still in Czechoslovakia. We were greatly surprised to see that the Russians were there already, ahead of us. They seemed to have been waiting for us with their tanks, their weapons, and their self-satisfied grins.

They had conquered the Nazis, which meant we could be considered their friends, but we were Germans for the Czechs and for the Russians, since we were from the Sudetenland, and it remained to be seen how they would treat us. A Russian soldier signaled us to stop and, after looking us over and checking the car meticulously, shouted at us:

"Davay chasi! davay chasi!"

He was asking for our watches. Without a word or any resistance, we handed them over. The man grabbed the watches, looked at them, and signaled us to move on. The truck with the Jews followed us.

A few miles farther along we were stopped again, but this time they demanded the car. *"Motoren, Motoren,"* they said over and over. As I got out, I looked back and noticed that the truck with our friends had disappeared. I was so frightened that I did not realize that the only valuable possession we had left was inside the car: the diamond hidden under the right-side seat. I managed to grab only my black leather handbag.

It was a chaotic spectacle: people speaking different languages, not knowing where to go, walking around in total confusion. I kept saying to myself again and again that I could not afford to lose control, since Oskar seemed to be in a trance, in the same state of shock that had made him try to flee over unknown lands without the help of a map.

The Other Schindlers

AFTER CROSSING THE TANK EMPLACEMENT AREA, WE MET Annelie, who had been Oskar's lover when they were both with the Counterintelligence Service. A forlorn-looking couple was standing next to her, at the side of the road. The man had been wounded in the war, and his wife was a small, delicate woman. Curiously, they had our same last name, Schindler. The woman was carrying a Luger pistol in her handbag, similar to the one I had in Märisch Ostrau, and I was very apprehensive of what would certainly happen to us if the Russians found it.

Suddenly, I heard a voice behind me calling my name. I quickly turned around: it was a Russian girl who had worked as a cook at the Brünnlitz factory.

"Frau Schindler!" she called, recognizing me. There was desperation in her voice. "What are you doing here? I haven't forgotten how good you always were to me, and I would like to help you. I'll try to make an arrangement with the Russians so that you and your husband can spend the night in a truck without being bothered. You can have confidence in me."

Stories about the abuses committed by the Russian troops against the civilian population made people fear the worst. There was not a woman, regardless of her age or looks, who was safe from being raped by the soldiers. And the Czechs were no better.

Just as the cook had promised, we were able to sleep in a truck. Oskar quickly found good company in a Russian soldier, together with whom he undertook the task of emptying a bottle of vodka. Drunk, they spent a good part of the night shouting "Long live Stalin!" My husband, of course, was no communist. He simply pretended, as he had done before with the Nazis, to be in agreement with the slogan of the day.

The next morning, a very well-dressed man approached us with the warning that the situation was getting more and more threatening. And if we owned anything of value, he would be happy to hide it for us in his home. We could pick it up when everything calmed down. Evidently, he was one of those trying to make a profit out of the total confusion. We politely told him that it would not be necessary; we had nothing left.

In just a few minutes, a group of Czech soldiers wanted to deliver us to the Russians. We resisted and succeeded in being sent to the Red Cross instead. Inside the tent, they were asking to search our bags to see whether we were really neutral. As soon as they opened the other Frau Schindler's handbag, they found the Luger. The Czechs determined she should be executed immediately. Her husband wailed desperately: "Don't kill her, please don't kill her." But the soldiers paid no attention to his pleas, firm in their decision to execute the poor woman.

They dragged her away. Then a shot was heard, and we saw the body of my namesake fall, covered with blood. The war was over, but the land was still bathed in terror. Death lurked everywhere, on either side, victory or defeat. Fifty years later, I am still tormented by that image.

Lost in the Waters

AFTER THAT INCIDENT, I BEGAN TO THINK ABOUT WHAT I HAD in my own black handbag, and held it tightly against my body, my hands trembling. It contained our documents and Annelie's. If the Czechs saw them, they would execute us immediately. I had to act quickly. I turned around and saw a canal a few feet away. Without any hesitation, I walked close to the water and, after looking right and left, hurled my handbag into the canal.

Although the Red Cross accepted us without major objections, we felt helplessly forsaken. Then suddenly, as if by a miracle, God took pity on us. A Czech soldier approached me and asked:

"Are you looking for your friends? I think they are sleeping in that room."

The Jews who had followed us in the truck were there, close to where we were now. They had told the Red Cross command what we had done for them.

As I was leaving the tent, my husband's shouts made me turn my head. He was standing with Annelie, next to an ambulance, and screaming as if possessed, repeating desperately: "They're going to shoot me, they're going to shoot me." I had no idea what was going on. When I was able to ask him, he said that he had heard a group of Russian soldiers say that they were looking for a certain Schindler of Mährisch Ostrau who had been with the Counterintelligence Service.

As I was trying to calm him down, a well-dressed man asked me where we were from. From the Sudetenland, I answered. He then warned me not to tell anybody else if we wanted to stay alive. We should therefore make an effort not to speak German in the presence of strangers.

When we finally got reunited with our friends, only seven remained of the eight who had left Brünnlitz. An eighteen-year-old girl who had been on the truck had vanished without a trace. Apparently she had fallen into Russian hands. I later heard she had been seen in Prague, several months pregnant, no doubt as a result of the many rapes she had been subjected to by the soldiers.

God's Hotel

TWO DAYS LATER, MEMBERS OF THE RED CROSS BROUGHT US to a hotel in Deutschbrod formerly favored by traveling salesmen. Only one heavily damaged wing of that great inn remained standing. Traude, Annelie, and I were assigned one room, together with other women. The men had to sleep in a large hall full of dust and rubble, which looked as if it had once been the hotel dining room.

I went into our room and saw a rickety chair, a small bed, an old dark armoire, a matching round table, and, on the table, an old book in red leather binding, which turned out to be a Bible. What was a Bible doing there? I opened it at random to a passage of the Book of Jeremiah:

> *For who shall have pity upon thee, O Jerusalem? or who shall bemoan thee? or who shall go aside to ask how thou doest? . . . Their widows are increased to me above the sand of the seas. . . . I have caused him to fall upon it suddenly, and terrors upon the city. . . . Woe is me, my mother, that thou hast borne me a man of strife and a man of contention to the whole earth!*

This is God's answer to the terrible words of the prophet:

> And I will deliver thee out of the hand of the wicked, and I will redeem thee out of the hand of the terrible.

Suddenly my hopes were reborn. In the midst of so much desolation, I had received a message. As the sky was turning darker, a strange radiance was brightening my heart, until then laden with somber thoughts by the feeling that all roads were being closed off to us, that there was no escape.

We stayed at the inn three days and three nights. Under specific orders from the Red Cross, Oskar was not allowed to go anywhere. Finally they took us to the train station, from which we were supposed to leave for the western front. The station had been totally demolished, as well as the other buildings in Deutschbrod, and of the main structure a single wall with a small window remained, through which you could see only nothingness.

We no longer had any points of reference; it did not matter much where we went. But Rizyard Rechen, one of the Jews who had journeyed with us in the truck, wanted to go to Switzerland because he had relatives there. We decided to join him.

On the Way

AT A SLOW PACE, THE OLD LOCOMOTIVE MANAGED A LABORED stop among the ruins of the station. We boarded in the middle of the night and looked for a place to sit. The train was not very long—it had only a few cars—and all the windows were broken. Suddenly the silence was interrupted by the whistle of the stationmaster, and the locomotive, wheels screeching on the rails, slowly started to pull the train away.

We were leaving Deutschbrod behind, the ruins of the old hotel, the dismantled train station, the canal whose waters had swallowed our identities. . . . The words of that Bible passage were still very much in my mind. The city behind us became smaller and smaller, and as we moved away and into the night, our entire life seemed to be vanishing. . . .

With the relief of leaving behind all the tension of those last days, and the clatter of the train, everybody began to fall asleep. I kept watching the people, trying to imagine what they were dreaming about. Oskar was sitting facing me and Oberek facing Traude, who was next to me, and a little behind us, Rizyard Rechen. Watching others sleep gave me a sense of peace. That feeling was not being communicated to me from their souls, but rather from their tired bodies, which for the first time in a long while had found a refreshing rest.

Suddenly Oskar rose, half asleep, and pulled the emergency brake with all his strength. The wheels screeched with a deafening sound, and the train dragged on slowly for a few more feet before coming to a halt. One of the train guards, rubbing his eyes, appeared in the still-dark aisle and asked sharply what had happened, and who was responsible for stopping the train. Someone in the Jewish group said that we all had been asleep. The guard, still without understanding what had triggered the incident, began to explain to us the correct functioning of the hand brake. Once his midnight lecture was over, he wished us good night and left. He was the epitome of a German bureaucrat.

As soon as he was gone, I confronted Oskar and, very annoyed, asked him what on earth he was trying to do. With a combination of regret and humility unusual in him, he told me that he was having a terrible nightmare: the train was going full speed down a steep slope with an abyss on each side, and he managed to stop it by pulling the hand brake, thus saving his life and that of the other passengers.

After a few hours of traveling, we arrived at the transfer point, where we would board the train to take us to Pilsen. The station was as demolished as the one we left behind in Deutschbrod. The only thing still standing was a cracked, huge platform.

Still in our summer clothes and light shoes, we had to wait all night, shivering in the cold, in that desolate place. We slept in one of the railroad cars that had brought us there, while rumors kept growing of the arrival of the Russian troops on their victorious march toward Berlin.

Suddenly, the car in which we were sleeping started to move, and after a short trip we arrived at another station. An incredible sight greeted us. The whole station was enveloped in a thick white cloud. When we tried to find out what it was, the guard explained that the Russians had found a freight train loaded with feather comforters. Looking for God knows what, they had hacked them to pieces with their knives and bayonets, spreading the contents all over and filling the station with goose feathers. In spite of our misery and desolation, the story made us, more than once, laugh out loud.

At last it was time to board our train to Pilsen. Very close to that city, world famous for its beer, the train stopped and to our horror a guard showed up to inform us that the engineer had received orders to take only the locomotive to Pilsen and leave the other cars behind for a few hours. He added that if we valued our lives at all, we should lie down on the floor of the railroad car because the soldiers would probably start shooting any minute.

Uncomfortable, starving, and freezing, we waited until five in the morning, when we heard the noises of the locomotive starting to rehitch the cars. I sat up slowly and tried to look out the window to see what was going on. A masculine voice jolted me:

"Out! Everybody out!"

Shelter

ONCE WE REACHED THE PLATFORM, WE WERE RECEIVED BY two young men in uniform who were speaking in English. God continued to be merciful to us. We had finally succeeded in reaching the western front.

While the American soldiers instructed us to board a bus, they kept repeating: "They are Jews. . . ." We were driven to a small town where several rows of tanks had been posted. Luckily, two of the Jewish men with us knew English and were able to communicate with the camp commander.

While we were waiting for their return from a meeting with the Americans, we had to stay with the bus. We had nothing to eat until five in the afternoon, when the two Jews returned with the commander. In the meantime, as if to make our wait even more difficult, we had to content ourselves with watching the American soldiers eat.

"Happy to welcome you" was the field commander's greeting. "I am really happy to welcome the first contingent of Jews."

By chance, Oskar and I had been included in the group, and happily nobody bothered to contradict the words of the U.S. officer. The commander, a pleasant-looking young man, said that his name was Klein and that he was also Jewish. . . . We all were!

On one of my latest trips to the United States, I met Commander Klein again. In spite of the years gone by, he still had the special shine in his eyes that had given us the feeling we were home at last. He welcomed me again as he had done then, and added: "I have not forgotten you, Mrs. Schindler."

Klein took us to general headquarters, where we were allowed to wash up and have something to eat. I shall never

forget the taste of that wonderful soup, the first thing we had
to eat in three days. We had to get some empty tin cans first,
wash them, and use them as soup dishes. After we ate and
rested for a while, the Americans asked us where we wanted
to go. Almost in unison, we answered: "To Switzerland."

In the same friendly manner as before, they assigned a
small bus to us and gave us a series of passes to obtain gas
along the way. We said good-bye and began our journey to
Switzerland, which had remained neutral during the war,
with hopes of starting a new life, but still harboring in our
hearts the fear that this was but one more step in our never-
ending attempt to escape. To enter a foreign country, being
German, involved a great risk, but we had no other alternative.

We reached a small town where we took a train for
Constance, Switzerland. From the window I could see the
beautiful mountain peaks rising high on the horizon. I mar-
veled at the cultivated fields and their great variety of colors.
I again felt the breath of freedom on my skin. The war was
over, and this was not an illusion.

In Constance, after getting off the train, we were taken to
a hotel where lunch was ready for us. For a second time in
two days we could satisfy our hunger. Arranged on a huge
table there were various bowls filled with potato dumplings
and green salads. Large pitchers of coffee and tea were
served with the abundant meal.

After we recovered our strength, Oskar decided it was
time to initiate some contacts that would allow us to
improve our lot. A week later he went to the American zone
in Bavaria to find out what the future offered us and to figure out which direction to take. During that time the Jews in
our group were leaving for different destinations, depending
on where they had been able to obtain residency permits.
Some went to South America, others to the United States or

Australia, places where refugees were more easily accepted.

Only the four of us stayed in Switzerland: Oskar, his niece Traude, Annelie, and I.

Regensburg

THREE MONTHS LATER, IN OCTOBER 1945, OSKAR RETURNED from Munich, proudly waving passes to the American sector. They had cost him a great deal of energy and patience; the negotiations were not easy at all. In Munich he had contacted the American administration through the Jewish Council.

Again we were at a railroad station, this time waiting for a train to Ulm. The trip was a disaster. The railroad cars were in very bad condition, with all the windows and doors broken. It was the beginning of fall, and we were still wearing our light summer clothes. We felt the cold in our bones.

In Ulm we had to change to another train. Our lives seemed to consist now of endless waiting at desolate, ramshackle train stations. Behind us was the famous old cathedral of Ulm, half in ruins. Nothing else was still standing in what had once been a beautiful city. The same desolate landscape greeted us in Munich, where we spent the night with some people we knew.

Through Joint, the Jewish organization that had taken part in drawing up the list, we were assigned an apartment in Regensburg, a city under American administration. It was a fairly large, five-room house, with a beautiful kitchen and a huge bathroom, quite beyond our needs and expectations. Once a month, Joint sent us a food package that we opened with trembling fingers, eager to find out what it contained: flour, cigarettes, coffee, tea, sugar—items that were like gold toward the end of 1945. The black market was active everywhere, and I exchanged whatever I could on the streets.

Life in Regensburg, which is known as Ratisbona in some parts of the world, was not at all easy. Its inhabitants did not look kindly on strangers like us who had some of the food items that they themselves often could not obtain. They did not treat us well and always made us feel like strangers. This was not an unreasonable reaction if you consider that, after suffering in the war for six years, people were not eager to share anything, much less with second-class Germans coming from the Sudetenland. Of course, there was not much to share, but what seemed to bother them the most was having to live with people they considered inferior.

Once during a walk with Annelie, someone emptied from a window a bucket of some foul-smelling liquid on us; I'd rather not think about what it was. I interpreted it as part insult and part purification: since we were not entirely Aryan, we were "savages" that had to be cleansed.

A German minister made sure we knew that we were not welcome in "his" city. He even walled the door to a bathroom when he found out that we were using it. From a family house in a nearby field, came the tantalizing warm aroma of freshly baked bread. But when we tried to buy it or exchange it for something else, we were told, without any regard whatsoever for the value of the money or merchandise we were offering, that the baked bread was for the exclusive consumption of the German people.

This situation irritated me. At some point I got the idea of buying grapes to resell on the black market. This way we could make some money to buy the things we needed at a store owned by a Jewish family. After learning the story of our lives, they were the only ones willing to do business with us.

Annelie and I took a very crowded train to the wine region, not very far from Regensburg. After a long walk we reached the vineyards. The green vines and the luscious grapes were really tempting. We looked for the owner, who was busy restoring his place. We said hello and asked if we could buy two large bags of grapes. His immediate reply was that grapes would only leave his place in the form of wine. From inside the house we heard a woman's voice:

"Hans, if they are not Germans, don't sell them wine either."

I was so outraged I did not say a word. Annelie and I walked around the area until it was dark. We went by the vineyard where we had been treated so shabbily, and an idea took hold of me. If they would not sell us the grapes, we had to steal them. We started to cut some bunches, and then we filled the two bags we had brought with us.

At the station we had to wait almost all night for the train. With all that waiting time and the time the trip itself took, many of the grapes almost turned into raisins, and we were able to sell only half of our harvest.

From then on, we decided to exchange grapes for apples or pears. But it seemed that I was the only one to take care of practical matters. On one occasion I had to stay at the hospital in Regensburg because of my chronic pain. Traude and Annelie came to see me, and they had with them a few bags of apples, but when both fell asleep, they were robbed and lost them all.

The only reliable source of income we had was the then famous CARE packages, which owed their name to an organization created in Berlin by the American administration, called Cooperative for American Remittances to Europe. The longed-for box came once a month and usually contained powdered eggs or powdered milk, chocolate, coffee, tea, and sugar. Some of those products ended up on the black market, where I exchanged them for something more substantial.

The Lost Child

AT FIRST OUR LIFE IN REGENSBURG SEEMED TO HERALD A NEW beginning and the return of happiness to our marriage. On our first nights together Oskar again became the ardent lover concerned about his partner's pleasure that he had been at the beginning. I started to think that after all the life we had shared during the war, it was possible to think of our future.

One evening, while we were at the movies watching a romantic film, I felt a terrible pain in my lower abdomen. At first I tried to pay no attention to it, but it became more and more unbearable and I developed a high fever. We rushed to the town hospital, where I was admitted right away.

An operation was performed the following day. I had a dead baby inside of me. As a result of that operation, I could no longer think of having children of my own.

Still in pain and under the influence of anesthesia, I opened my eyes and saw Oskar's smiling face. To my surprise, he was not alone. His companion was Gisa, his lover, whom he would later drag along with him to Argentina. In my condition I could not really grasp what was happening, but I felt a tremendous letdown in every fiber of my body.

I wept disconsolately. As I began to understand the real situation, I blamed myself for having believed that Oskar could ever change. Then I remembered the rumor that had circulated in Brünnlitz about two children, allegedly his, the product of his affair with the daughter of a Zwittau police officer.

I recently found out that the son is at present living in Australia. His mother mistreated him terribly, and he was not quite normal. He used to wander aimlessly through the streets of the town, left to his own devices and eccentric behavior.

My Last Image of Franz

TOWARD THE END OF 1945, WALKING AROUND REGENSBURG, I bumped into my brother. According to my parents' last will, the land and the house at Alt Moletein belonged to Franz, but the war had forced him to abandon them. I learned from him that the Pelzls no longer had any possessions, only the memory of how our life had been and of what was once ours.

He looked very ill, and Annelie took care of him. She attended to his needs personally, as the state of my own health prevented me from doing much for him. I had acquired a lung infection back at Brünnlitz that now required frequent and painful suction of fluids.

Oskar tried to help my brother by getting him a farm job, which was the kind of work he was used to doing. Franz replied that he was tired of farm labor and that someone had offered him a job as street caretaker. It was clearly evident that he wanted a change in his life. He had become a sullen and whining person with whom it was almost impossible to hold a sustained conversation. My husband persisted, but could not persuade him to return to his former country life.

As soon as Franz recovered, he stayed with my sister-in-law Elly, Oskar's sister, but we soon lost track of him.

My husband was the last one to see him. We were living at 24 Nürnbergerstrasse, on the east side of the Danube, and to get to the other side you had to take a little boat because the bridge had been hit by bombs and was dangerously near collapse. There were other passable bridges, but they were far away. Crossing over in the boat one morning, Oskar recognized him. Franz was washing his clothes on the shore. Shortly afterward, he disappeared from my sister-in-law's house.

We never heard from him again.

Money and Love

THINGS BEGAN TO IMPROVE IN 1947 WITH THE ANNOUNCE-ment of the so-called Marshall Plan. When Oskar found out about this plan, he left again for Munich to contact people who might be able to help us rebuild our lives.

The Rossners, a Jewish family now in the United States, then lived in Munich. There they reestablished my husband's contact with Joint, which gave Oskar about fifteen thousand dollars in recognition of what he had done for the Jews during the war.

But the travails of war did not make Oskar more austere: he spent the money on small pleasures and on objects for which we had not the slightest need. I never saw a penny of what he received. What is more, I found out about the Joint money only much later . . . and long after Oskar had spent a large part of it with one of his girlfriends during a relaxing vacation in the mountains, while my niece Traude and I had to perform miracles in order to obtain enough food on the black market.

It was useless to expect Oskar to change. That was impossible for him. In spite of the difficult circumstances, he continued, like a child, to follow his whims and, when it came to important decisions, to cling desperately to me, his refuge in times of crisis.

I had often considered the possibility of leaving him, of starting a new life without him, without his lies, without his repeated deceits and constant insincere repenting. But my religious ideas, my belief in God and the teachings of the Church, dissuaded me from doing so.

Besides, I had lost everything: home, country, family. My parents were dead, and my brother, whom I had last seen in 1946, had gone his own way. I had no choice but to adapt, to tighten my lips and close my eyes to Oskar's neglect and indifference. I shed many bitter tears because of him, but in time I toughened up. I stopped crying and immersed myself in my work.

Emilie, the woman, the lover, was fading into oblivion at a slow, sad pace. The love I had felt for my husband gradually eroded, and outwardly I was becoming dry and distant. However, I am like the Sabras, the natives of Israel: on the outside they seem hard and insensitive, but inside they are sweet and sincere, like the fruit of the cactus growing in the desert in which they live.

On the Way to America

WE STAYED IN REGENSBURG FOR FIVE LONG YEARS, RESIGNED to our fate in the midst of postwar chaos. In 1949 our lives were to change radically. After a long stay in Munich, Oskar returned with the news that he had two passes, provided by Joint, to embark on the last ship that would take Jewish refugees to South America. Our original plan was to settle in Paraguay, but at the last moment Oskar preferred Argentina because he had some acquaintances there. I was not over-joyed at the news, although I did look forward to moving to a different place.

We had few belongings, so no great preparations were necessary. We said good-bye to Traude and set out for Genoa, port of departure for the ship that was to take us to Buenos Aires, the capital of Argentina. The name of the city sounded exotic and filled me with great curiosity. When I found out what it meant [good air], I thought it was particu-larly appropriate for a place that had become a refuge for so many people fleeing from horror. However, I later learned that in those years many former members of the Nazi high command had arrived at this same port through an organization called ODESSA, escaping in this manner their well-deserved punishment.

On a cold October morning we boarded a ship flying the Swiss flag. Besides us and a small group of twelve Jews, there was a large group of Italians, mostly from the south, who were escaping joblessness and starvation.

An Infernal Voyage

IT TOOK US TWENTY-EIGHT DAYS TO CROSS THE ATLANTIC.

We traveled amid bundles of clothes and with children running around in the ship's corridors. There were separate cabins for the men and for the women, but night visits were frequent. During the day the bow was the only place to be, though it was also crowded with people moving from one end of the ship to the other in order to kill time.

Sanitary measures were practically nonexistent. The stench from the bathrooms carried quite a distance. The situation worsened when we reached the point where the Mediterranean and the Atlantic meet. The ship pitched and rolled incessantly, rocking at the whim of huge waves that pounded the deck. Passengers were throwing up everywhere, seasick from the ship's roll. Under those conditions it was impossible to eat anything. I lost over twenty pounds during this voyage, in less than a month.

We began to notice changes in climate. Days were turning sunnier and warmer. We had left Genoa in the fall, which in Buenos Aires was spring, and this filled me with optimism in spite of the dreadful voyage. To arrive at a new country when everything is starting to bloom and life renews itself could only be interpreted as a favorable omen. Before falling asleep on the hard cot assigned to me, I imagined that everything would change and that my life would start all over again, but differently.

And yet, these happy daydreams could not dispel the terrible nightmares I had as soon as I fell asleep. I dreamed that the Nazis were persecuting me for having helped the Jews. When I woke up, drenched in sweat, I asked myself how much longer I would have to live in such desperation, such anguish, such fear in my soul.

Finally the day came when we heard over the loudspeakers: "Ladies and gentlemen, tomorrow we arrive in Buenos Aires, Republic of Argentina." This was announced first in Italian, then in English. Although I spoke neither of those two languages, I understood that our voyage was coming to an end. Sighting the port brought us pure joy. In this happiness we all felt united—Germans, Jews, and Italians.

I quickly went down to my cabin and began packing my few belongings. I was impatient to face what would be my new homeland.

PART FIVE

A New Home

In Good Health

THE FIRST THING I SAW FROM THE DECK WAS the skyline of the city, reflected in the brown waters of the River Plate. A bunch of sea gulls circled above as if welcoming us. The landscape, so full of movement and at the same time strangely peaceful, impressed me so much that I could not help feeling emotional, and involuntary tears streamed down my face.

We landed in Buenos Aires on November 3, 1949. Dragging our luggage, we had to go through the quarantine office, where immigrants were subjected to a meticulous medical examination. In this respect, the requirements of the Argentinean authorities were absolutely clear and unwavering: to be allowed into the country one had to be in perfect health.

A crowd had gathered outside the provisional medical office, set up precariously in the customs building. The tense, anguished expression on the faces of those waiting gave testimony to the fear that any disease might cause them to be sent back to Europe.

Ahead of us was a couple with three small children. The woman was very beautiful, with huge, dark eyes and long, shiny, jet-black hair. The whole family had that special bearing of southern Europeans. They entered together, and fifteen minutes later we heard, in a language unfamiliar to me, the husband screaming, which could only mean that, for some reason, the Argentinean authorities had denied them a residency permit. When he came out through the small door, the man walked in desperation toward a police officer and, falling to his knees, shouted: *"Pietá, pietá!"*

After that distressing incident and the admission of a group of Jews, it was our turn, Oskar's and mine. Fortunately we had no problem. The authorities checked our documents over and over and looked at us as if they wanted to discover something that our passports would not reveal. They talked among themselves, but I could understand only a reference to our homeland, though the word *Alemania* sounded very different from *Deutschland*.

Having completed the required procedures, we went to a hotel on Corrientes Street on the recommendation of a man who had come with the Jewish group. Someone his family knew, who had managed to emigrate in 1936 before the war began, had stayed there.

We split into groups and went to the hotel in three taxis. I remember they were all Mercedes-Benzes, which for a moment made me feel we were still in Germany.

I'll never forget my first impressions as we drove through the streets of Buenos Aires, to me such a new and different city. None of us said a word during the taxi ride; we just looked out the windows: the Plaza de Mayo, the Government Palace (Casa Rosada), painted an indefinable shade of pink and surrounded by the various cabinet buildings, the banks, and the cathedral, where the remains of the great national hero, General San Martín, were laid to rest. Facing the Casa Rosada, we discovered the old Cabildo building, a Spanish colonial landmark, magnificently white with green iron gratings and green doors, all so very different from what I was accustomed to. Here there were no traces of war. Everything was spacious, crystal-clear, and peaceful.

We then crossed the huge avenue with the Obelisk, symbol of the city of Buenos Aires. Everything communicated a happy and positive feeling, except for Oskar's face, which seemed to say that he was watching a movie he had no interest in seeing, and was eager to go somewhere else.

Our hotel was near the Obelisk. It was an old building with the reception desk at the top of a long staircase. It made a good impression on me, though not precisely for being luxurious or overly clean. The price seemed modest, it was reasonably comfortable, and the food was delicious and plentiful, something our European stomachs had been missing for a long time.

The concierge welcomed us with a smile and words that appeared to be of greeting, though none of us were able to understand them fully, so we interpreted them as a welcome and let him carry our luggage to our rooms. I realized that I would have to learn Spanish and decided to do so quickly, as I had previously done with Polish and Czech.

In San Vicente

OSKAR RAPIDLY ESTABLISHED CONTACTS WITH THE JEWISH community in Argentina. He was introduced to an industrialist who had just bought a farmhouse in the area of San Vicente. When he offered us the job of caretakers, we did not have to think much about it. I was familiar with farm work, and the opportunity to work again under an open sky, after so many years of living in cities and dark factories, sounded like an attractive proposition.

We accepted at once, and soon we were settled in San Vicente, a small town almost forty miles from Buenos Aires. The population was of Italian and Spanish descent, living simply and working hard.

The center of San Vicente, where I have lived to this day, is not very impressive. Everything revolves around the main plaza, surrounded by the Bank of the Province of Buenos Aires, the army post, and a few stores. The old church, with its brown-gray hues and its easily recognizable colonial style, rises above the town skyline. Its two round towers remind me of south German architecture. Several ancient trees surround the plaza and fill it with beautiful colors, especially when they are covered with flowers in the summer.

At the time we arrived at San Vicente, most farmhouses (known as quintas) had been built on lands devoted to fruit trees and livestock. Perón, who was then president of the country, had a huge quinta in San Vicente, not very far from where I am living now. In those times there were only dirt roads, and driving in and out of the quintas each time it rained became a big problem.

Not far from town is the Ezeiza international airport. The noise of aircraft always accompanies us, but in time one is no longer aware of it.

Our job at Quinta San Vicente was raising chickens and egg-laying hens. At first it was rather tough: I did not know the language and had to adapt to a country with customs very different from mine, all in addition to never-ending chores. I started taking care of the poultry at five in the morning, all year round. I checked everything, placed fresh water in the small drinking dishes, and mixed grains with corn. Then I had to collect, sort, and carefully clean the eggs before finally placing them in cartons to be sent to the market. Once a day, I made myself a hot meal, did the household chores, and returned to the hens.

This routine lasted eight uninterrupted years. I could not count on help from Oskar, who seemed more interested in the adventures the capital could provide.

One day he arrived at the quinta with one of his bright ideas. We would (Oskar always spoke in the plural) raise otters for their fur. I tried to dissuade him in every way possible, but when Oskar believed that one of his schemes could make money, no one could change his mind. I explained to him a thousand times that we did not have the slightest idea of how to raise otters, and warned him that he would get bored in a few days and that I would then be saddled with the difficult task of taking care of the animals. But it was all to no avail, so I had to immerse myself in the life of otters.

The Otters

THE FOLLOWING DAY I TOOK THE FIRST MORNING TRAIN TO Buenos Aires, to canvass various bookstores so that I could arm myself with knowledge about otters, which up to then I had seen more on the shoulders of Oskar's lovers than on my own.

After purchasing a few books recommended as the best on the subject, I went into a little bar on Corrientes Street, asked for a double coffee, lit a cigarette, and started to leaf through them. I discovered that otters live on all the continents except South America. The animals offered to Oskar were really nutrias [coypus]. Once I was informed of their genealogy and habits, I got ready to receive them. They arrived in a truck, all crammed together in big metal cages.

Oskar called me as soon as they were in, and with a big smile he said to me:

"Emilie, behold before you the business of the century. We're going to be millionaires. All the women wear fur coats."

I agreed, but thought to myself that I was still the exception to that rule. I also knew that Oskar's enthusiasm concealed the most important fact: that whether otters or nutrias, it was I, and I alone, who was going to take care of them.

I had exchanged hens for mammals, but the time schedule for the needed tasks was still the same, from daybreak till sundown. My husband was always busy elsewhere.

Oskar's Love Affairs

WHEN I WAS WALKING IN TOWN OR ATTENDING SOME GET-together, I used to look at all the women and ask myself with which ones and with how many of them had Oskar had affairs. The answer became easier over time: surely with all those who would allow it. The interesting thing was that these conquests required no effort on his part. With his natural seductiveness, it was the women who were constantly after him.

Not so long ago, during a press conference, a Spanish newspaperwoman asked me if Oskar was really as good-looking as Liam Neeson, the actor who played him in *Schindler's List*. I smiled, thinking of his elegant bearing, handsome looks, blond hair, lively and intensely blue eyes, plus a smile that became quite seductive unintentionally. . . . And I knew that again, I would chose Oskar.

I was also reminded of the strong, masculine smell of his body, and I felt like denying all that has been said, in the film and in books, about the perfumes he wore, when, as a matter of fact, all he ever used was aftershave lotion. The newspaperwoman was still waiting for a reply, but I preferred to leave the question up in the air and just smiled.

Of course, I was not the only one who had really fallen for

him. Oskar was aware that women noticed him, and he seemed to feel an obligation to play his part in these casual affairs. But once he got involved—and this he confessed to me more than once when, repentant, he came back to my arms—he did not know how to break free.

To my constant reproaches, he would reply:

"Look, Emilie, we all have to follow our nature. We have to live in the moment, and everything else comes by itself, no matter what we may have planned or expected."

Whenever I heard his peculiar version of carpe diem, I could not help remembering some of his family's character traits. The least desirable of Oskar's traits came from his father. His father was a hopeless alcoholic who, in one of his awful drinking binges, raped his wife's sister and got her pregnant. From that brutal union, a beautiful girl was born, but she died at fourteen, while scarcely an adolescent.

As Oskar's father, he was not very affectionate either. Shortly after Oskar's seventeenth birthday, his father accused him of a theft he had not committed, and Oskar had a taste of what it meant to live behind bars. His father had been selling insurance, and when faced with some financial difficulties, he decided to keep the money from the premiums. When the police questioned him, he could find no better way to avoid going to jail himself than to blame his own son.

The Zwittau house belonged to Oskar's mother. One day his father came home with a mortgage in one hand and a huge cake in the other. Whenever he took a false step, caused some serious trouble, or got drunk, he used to bring home a cake. We never could tell whether it was a cover-up . . . or part of his celebration.

In any case, my husband's regrets were those of a better man. He knew that what he was doing was wrong, that he was hurting me, but he couldn't change. Oskar suffered every time he left one of his lovers. I would see him come home, sad-eyed and with a lost look on his face, as if he regretted being no longer able to give himself to the woman he was abandoning. In spite of my irritation, I saw him as a boy, as a victim of his own mischief.

That is what Oskar was, a boy. However, in his dealings with the SS high command, he was at once engaging and determined.

Concerning his infidelities, I found it hardest to understand why he generally got involved with ugly, vulgar, lower-class women.

Shortly before the onset of the war, while Oskar was working for the Counterintelligence Service, he had to go to another city and stay at a hotel. I don't exactly remember why, but the fact is that I had to travel to that city to bring him some papers he had forgotten at home. When I asked for Oskar, the doorman, who already knew me, said:

"It's a pleasure to see you here, Frau Schindler, but your husband has already left, and not alone."

Relinquishing all diplomacy and all modesty, I daringly asked him with whom had my husband left. The man hesitated a few moments and then tried to explain, in a very roundabout way, that there had been a scandal at the hotel. Oskar and his lover, in the heat of sexual ecstasy, had broken the bed. My shame was much greater than my surprise, as I was very well aware of my husband's amorous talents.

Gisa

THE STRANGEST THING OF ALL WAS THAT OSKAR'S INFIDELITIES had the approval and collaboration of some of our best friends. When we passed through Munich after the war, we stayed with a Jewish family who had been with us at Brünnlitz.

The woman had a friend named Gisa, then a fairly common Jewish nickname. Oskar quickly started a liaison with her. The affair flourished with the help of the lady of the house, who provided a room for Oskar and Gisa to enjoy their romantic union whenever my husband went to Munich with the excuse of having to take care of some business. What Oskar did not tell me when he brought the tickets for South America was that Gisa would be coming with us. When I found out, just before packing, I did not have the energy for futile reproaches anymore. As absurd as it may seem, I clung to the hope that once in Argentina, I would again be Oskar Schindler's only woman. It proved to be a false hope.

Fortunately, we moved to San Vicente, which offered as its main advantage that it was quite far from the Belgrano neighborhood, where the inevitable Gisa lived. She used my husband for all he was worth, made him give her jewelry and even an authentic otter coat. When he returned to Germany for good, Gisa felt forsaken and wrote letters to him full of reproaches. One day I received a few lines from Oskar asking me to speak to her and try to persuade her to stop her epistolary insults, and to tell her that if she kept threatening him, he would never come back to her.

In my lifetime I had tolerated many of Oskar's humiliations, but this letter went too far. I did not, of course, do what he asked me, nor did I ever mention Gisa again in my letters.

The Separation

BEFORE I REALIZED IT, I HAD SPENT ALMOST EIGHT YEARS IN the routine of taking care of nutrias and feeding chickens. In 1957 the German government enacted a law providing that every victim of Nazism who had been affected by the loss of property, capital, or profession during World War II had the right to a reparation.

While in San Vicente, we received a letter requesting our presence in Germany in order to establish the amount of reparation due for the Brünnlitz factory. We were entitled to approximately two percent of the total value, which amounted to a sizable sum, considering the hardships we were suffering in Argentina.

After discussing the situation in detail, we agreed that Oskar would go to Germany. I would stay and work in San Vicente, and he would return with the money to pay off our debts, since the nutria business proved not to be as profitable, by far, as my husband had once imagined.

At first Oskar did not want to travel alone. Finally he agreed and promised to return as soon as all arrangements had been completed. I sensed that something might happen. I did not, however, realize the importance of his long history of infidelities, less-than-open money dealings, and lies that had marked our lives together, destroying a love that was supposed to have lasted forever. . . . Resigned, I accepted his words.

I had met him on a Thursday, I married him on a Thursday, and on a Thursday I saw him leave forever. In the spring of 1957 Oskar left Argentina, never to return. We hardly spoke a word on the way to the airport. Had we nothing to say to each other after sharing our lives for almost thirty years? Had all the suffering and hardship we had endured not served to bond us together? Had we grown that far apart?

We were very much in love when we married, but were too different in temperament. Oskar was not entirely a bad husband, but his fickleness and infidelities had already made an understanding between us impossible. He subordinated his duties to his desires, and that I could neither understand nor accept.

With the perspective of time, I now see our long marriage

as a kind of miracle. Maybe for Oskar it was just a comfortable habit. . . . It never interfered with what he wanted to do. In fact, being married to me often helped him get what he wanted. I stopped trusting him a long time before; he had ceased to be the person with whom I could share my joys and my sorrows.

That silence revealed the sad reality of our situation. I would have wanted Oskar, at least then, to have a moment of sincerity, his last opportunity to be truthful with me. But none of that happened. He said good-bye avoiding my eyes. He looked down as he passed through the gate, his suitcase dragging behind.

Watching his back as he walked away gave me a peculiar sensation. He was a complete stranger and, at the same time, a part of myself that was leaving me. I did not quite know to whom or to what I was bidding farewell.

I returned to the quinta and in anger kicked one of the cages. The otter, or the nutria, the difference did not matter anymore, shook herself sleepily and cuddled up again in a corner. As the days went by, an unfamiliar anxiety began to take hold of me, a tangible emptiness that seemed to be expanding.

Fiercely, I buried myself in work.

My Financial Struggles

MY FINANCIAL SITUATION WAS GETTING PROGRESSIVELY WORSE. I did not have enough money to pay the people helping me. At first they agreed to take eggs, animals, or fruit as wages. The last worker left one wintry afternoon:

"Doña Emilia, I am sorry. I can't go on working under these conditions. I have a family to support and need the money. You were always very good to me, and I am very sorry I have to leave you. Good-bye, Doña Emilia, and God bless you."

With head lowered, he disappeared beyond the gate into the approaching dusk.

I found myself facing the whole expanse of the quinta, about ten acres, with only one pair of hands. I had no money, my knowledge of Spanish was very limited, I missed having a man by my side, and day by day I was getting deeper into debt. I owed a million pesos, which then was quite a considerable sum, without any hope of ever being able to repay it. So there I was, surrounded by animals with which I could not talk, but which loudly demanded to be fed.

Had I gained anything by leaving postwar Europe, or was my list of misfortunes inevitably bound to repeat itself? I am well aware that revealing this side of my story may suggest that I am looking for sympathy. Nothing could be further from the truth. It is just that when I remember the desperation I felt in those days, even now I fail to understand how the mechanisms of justice work in this world. Today I am received by statesmen or I speak before thousands of people, but then my loneliness was so absolute that I don't know how I was able to bear it. The nights would stretch into long, endless periods of brooding in which I reviewed the past, analyzed the present, and tried to imagine some kind of future. Only dark, distressing shadows inhabited my mind, and more than once daylight woke me up, still in the kitchen, my head cradled in my arms.

My meals consisted of tangerines I picked in the orchard, some bread, and lots of coffee to keep me awake so I could take care of the nutrias, chickens, geese, dogs, and cats. That fare, with its mixture of sour and bitter tastes, inevitably reminded me of the abundant dinners I had enjoyed in my parents' home.

Once a week I went with my small savings to a nearby butcher's shop and bought liver for my dogs. As I entered the shop, the butcher would inevitably say: "Here comes the liver lady." That is how I was known in San Vicente for a long time. Back at home, I would dice the liver and distribute the little pieces in the style of Solomon: twenty pieces for each of my three dogs.

Burnt Letters

OSKAR'S LETTERS CAME VERY SPORADICALLY AND SEEMED copies of one another. They amounted to a lot of excuses, delays, and confused stories, without the slightest reference to my repeated pleas for help and to the difficult situation in which he had left me. Only once did he send any money, two hundred German marks, together with the *Diary of Anne Frank*. I chose not to think about whether he was trying to tell me something.

Little by little, his indifference and his lack of real answers were wearing out my determination to wait for him. Every time I wrote to him, I swore to myself that it would be the last time, until one day I finally kept my word. Oskar, nevertheless, continued writing. Whenever I saw an envelope with a German stamp, I would throw it into the fire, unopened.

A strange premonition held me back from burning his last letter, though. Knowing that I was living in poverty, he wrote this: *"My dear Emilie . . . I am gaining weight every day eating a lot of lobster and drinking a lot of good wine."* Why such cruelty? As far as I knew, I had never harmed him in any way or ever worked against his interests. I never did understand him. . . . Only God knows how often I tried.

I felt Oskar was responsible for my situation. I was supporting myself by selling milk from the cows I milked myself every morning. Each day, I covered ten miles to bring them hay I got from General Perón's quinta. But I loved those poor cows, and I said good night to them every evening before going to bed, always aware that I owed my survival to them. Today, when I see my dog Chupi and my badly injured cats—never fewer than twenty—I feel that throughout my life animals have been the best of companions.

I always managed to begin each day with renewed strength. It was like one of those secret miracles you create for yourself, with the help of God. Many years went by under these conditions. Over time, miracles cease to surprise us; they seem natural, when there is nothing natural about them. You struggle, you overcome, you struggle again, without knowing when everything will come to an end.

Meanwhile, Oskar in Germany received a hundred thousand marks in compensation for the Brünnlitz factory, as I later found out from acquaintances. But, of course, I never saw a penny of it. Knowing that he had received the money, and that he did not think of me, angered and saddened me even more. It raised questions not only about the present but about our past as well. Had I become a stranger to Oskar, or had I always been one?

Oskar's Business Dealings

NO ONE KNEW WHAT OSKAR DID WITH THAT MONEY. IN SPITE of his eagerness to make a fortune, his only business success was the enamelware factory in Cracow. When we were living in Regensburg, he was offered the management of a garage, certainly not a difficult job. But when a friend insinuated that such an occupation would be humiliating for Herr Direktor Schindler, my husband rejected a job that would have been a great help during those difficult times.

He also received a good job offer in Argentina: buying and

selling cinder blocks for prefabricated houses. It appeared to
be an easy job, and Oskar invested a considerable amount of
money in it, sixty thousand pesos, which he took out of our
savings. He did not have time to recover his investment. A
year and a half later, he let the business hang, and soon after
that he left for Germany.

An opportunity had also come my way. On a Sunday afternoon in 1952, a group of acquaintances had come to our
quinta for coffee. Card games quickly got started: one for the
men and one for the women, which Oskar of course joined,
as usual. I did not take part, because I was not interested. I
could never understand how people can waste so much time
with just some pieces of colored cardboard.

One of the visitors, a very wealthy Polish Jew who did not
seem to care about the card game either, asked me why I was
not playing. I said that I preferred to do some chore around
the house. When he heard my reply, he smiled and suggested that we relax on a couple of wicker chairs somewhat
removed from where the guests were playing.

It was a beautiful day, sunny and cool. The man said he
knew very well who I was and about my work ethic, my perse-
verance and punctuality. He told me there was a huge quinta,
not too far from ours, owned by an American who used it only
on weekends. The owner was planning to sell it, and he wanted to buy it so that I could manage a nutria farm. I was free,
moreover, to use the remainder of the 250 acres any way I
wanted, either cultivating the land or raising livestock.

He seemed quite determined to persuade me. However, I
had already had enough talk about nutrias with my husband.
While I listened to this man, I began picturing my situation:
alone, in such a big place, and surrounded by many more of
those creatures in which, in those days, everyone saw a
never-ending source of wealth. The results actually were far
less grand.

And as far as Oskar was concerned, I saw that none of this suited him, for despite his country upbringing, which was just like mine, he was decidedly a city person. His habitual inattentiveness, for example, caused the death of a beautiful female dog we had in San Vicente. Though I had warned him to be careful with the ant poison, he never paid any attention. One morning, the dog did not come to greet me. She was lying under a tree, poisoned. The vet came, but it was too late.

With this memory and others fresh in my mind, I rejected the offer, which, after Oskar's departure, would have made my years in Argentina more bearable.

Luckily someone informed the Jewish organization B'nai B'rith of my situation. One afternoon in the fall of 1963, several men in dark suits came to my San Vicente home, took stock of the situation, and a few days later returned with this advice: sell the quinta and pay off the debts with the proceeds. The proceeds from the sale just about covered my debts, but there was not a penny left to start anew. I was no longer a young woman, I was fifty-six, and, as they say in this part of the world, I was *con una mano atrás y otra delante* [destitute: with nothing on and trying to cover oneself].

As the Years Go By

SUDDENLY, WHEN I LEAST EXPECTED IT, I FOUND OUT THAT I had more friends than I thought.

The president of B'nai B'rith, Dr. Heinemann, assigned to me a house in San Vicente, where I still live and where I may stay until the day I die. I was also helped a great deal by Peter Gorlinsky, who died recently. He was a journalist with the *Argentinisches Tageblatt,* the daily newspaper of the

German community in Argentina, defender of the cause of freedom during the difficult war years.

In 1963 most newspapers and magazines in Germany published articles about Oskar, whom they called "Father Courage." The news reached Peter, who countered with an article entitled "Where Is Emilie Schindler, Mother Courage?" Thus he told the world that I was still alive. This brought the matter to the attention of the Jewish community, and some of its members saw to it that I received a small pension, which, together with money from my retirement and a subsidy from the German government, has allowed me to support myself to this day.

The year 1965 did not start off too well for me. I had a recurrence of my old back problem with increasing pain, made worse one day when I tried to lift a garden water pump. It might sound silly for a woman over sixty years old to attempt such a thing, but I had my reasons. That summer was especially hot, and therefore the lack of rain meant that the trees and the plants in the garden were so dry that they were threatening to die. One night, as a result of the frequent summer blackouts in San Vicente, the water pump broke.

The next day two electricians came, checked it, and told me it was beyond repair. The pump had burned out, and I needed a new one. I was so mad at this machine, which had failed me when I most needed it, that as soon as the men were gone, I tried to get it out of the way and throw it into some corner; it deserved no better.

It was then that I felt a sharp pain in my back, as if it were breaking in two, and I lost my balance. On hands and knees I managed to crawl to the bedroom and, with great effort, into my bed. I realized that my back had failed me again, and I could not get the fear out of my mind that I would never walk again.

I lay in bed for three months, not having enough money to pay for a doctor's visit, and dependent on the generosity of neighbors who kept house for me and brought me some things to eat. I slowly recovered, and as soon as I felt my strength returning, I resumed my chores.

I have always been a working woman, stubborn and industrious almost to the point of exaggeration, like a good peasant. Oskar claimed that my inability to relax and do nothing was a compulsion I continued to subject myself to because of my stubbornness. Must one first enslave oneself in order to be free? Or should one, as Oskar believed, surrender to one's inclinations? And what exactly were my own inclinations?

My mind roamed from one question to the next, but the everyday routine was much simpler: work, work, work. . . . No questions, no decisions. Is work the worst, or the best, way to struggle against oblivion? I don't know.

What I do know is that working until I was almost eighty had its physical consequences. My ulcers began to bleed again. This was an old wartime problem, elicited mainly by the constant situation of terror that Nazism had created.

This time the illness allowed me no reprieve. I lost so much blood that I had to be transferred right away to the German Hospital. The doctors were amazed that I had been able to survive, considering my condition. Of course, I had to stay hospitalized—for twenty-eight days.

There I was, the restless and tireless Emilie, confined to bed, with a weariness that apparently had been accumulating for years. I sought strength within me and could not find it. Is this what old age is, I asked myself, to know that you will never again be what you were? In the meantime, transfusion after transfusion, I slowly began to regain my health.

It was October, and I wanted to celebrate my birthday at

home. But I was not discharged in time. When the nurses and doctors found out, they arranged to get me a cake with a symbolic candle, which I blew out from my sickbed.

Dreaming About Alt Moletein

WITH SO MUCH TIME TO MYSELF, I COULD NOT HOLD BACK the thoughts revolving in my mind. If I had not met Oskar, how different would my life have been? What would have happened had I not accepted his marriage proposal? In what part of the world would I be, under which stars, in what latitude? All these questions plunged me into deep sadness, and, with tears streaming down my cheeks, I remembered with rare intensity the years of my childhood.

I was dreaming I was back home in Alt Moletein. It was the sixth of December and I was celebrating Saint Nicholas Day, surrounded by the love of my family. I again savored the taste of the roast turkey, my grandmother's specialty. But what I kept remembering most vividly was a holiday we used to celebrate on the first of May, following an old German custom, of planting a tree to keep the witches away. It felt as if I had returned to the place where my life had started. There, gone forever, were the seeds of my happiness or misfortune. . . . But now I was able to begin making choices all over again.

I would wake up realizing that such a thing was not possible, that time does not go backward. But dreaming of Alt Moletein nevertheless helped me to get through so many hours of loneliness.

Toward the end of October, the head physician of the German Hospital told me with a smile:

"Cheer up, Frau Schindler. Tomorrow you will be discharged. Try to take care of yourself when you are home. You can no longer work as you used to. You have to rest and recover."

The next day an ambulance left me at my doorstep. As I walked in, I felt disconnected. Everything was exactly where I had left it, and yet, there was something different but impossible to define. Maybe I had dreamed of that place so often that when I returned, nothing seemed exactly as I remembered it. Actually all the changes had occurred in myself. My strength was gone, and I could not resume the rhythm of my former life.

Emilie on the Screen

ONE GOOD DAY IN 1993 I RECEIVED A LETTER FROM STEVEN Spielberg inviting me to go to Jerusalem, with the necessary tickets enclosed. Very surprised, and with some misgivings, I contacted my friends in the Jewish community of Buenos Aires to find out what this was all about. They informed me that Spielberg was directing a film about Oskar and the list, the end of which he wanted to shoot in the Holy City with the actual survivors.

When I arrived in Israel, I met many of them, as well as their children and grandchildren. They were surprised that I was still alive and that I had settled in a small suburb in Argentina. It was not their fault that they did not know, but there were others in Los Angeles, whose names I would rather forget, who were very much aware of my existence and had made a lot of money selling the rights to the movie without any consideration for me whatsoever.

Reliving the past affected me spiritually and physically, to the point of my getting ill and requiring medical attention. That is why in the movie I appear in a wheelchair, while normally all I require to get around is a cane.

Spielberg again invited me to the *avant-première* in Washington, which was attended by President Bill Clinton and his wife, Hillary. I was seated behind people who were taller than me (which I must confess is not difficult), and I could hardly see anything. Shortly after it started, I fell asleep.

I was recently able to see the complete *Schindler's List*. Although based on a book that does not always reflect the whole truth, I thought it was an excellent film, and believe it well deserves all the awards it has received.

One segment that really bothered me was when Oskar is horseback riding with his lover by the entrance of the Cracow ghetto. Besides the bad taste of this scene, I must point out that the horses did not belong to the German army, as is suggested in Keneally's book, but had been purchased by my husband. The story bears telling.

The Polish countess of the house of von Haller had invited Oskar to her residence. She was in dire financial straits and needed money urgently. According to Oskar's report, a servant with threadbare white gloves served dinner, which consisted of potatoes in sour milk, and water as the only beverage. At the end of the frugal meal, the countess, without losing her aristocratic bearing, took my husband to the stables and sold him the animals in question. The horses were never much good for anything; they were old and did not stop eating, as if they had to make up for a lifetime of famine.

The film did not change my life much, except for the constant visits of reporters, always looking for news with which to fill their radio and television programs or pages in their newspapers and magazines. . . . Even though the film version is not entirely accurate, to be fair I must say that I owe to it the recognition that the world has finally given me.

At Oskar's Tomb

WHEN OSKAR ARRIVED IN GERMANY, HE SETTLED IN FRANKFURT, in a comfortable house on Bahnhofstrasse. He made several trips to Israel and to the United States, and even spent some time in Paris. For a while he directed a tile factory, which finally went bankrupt for reasons unknown to me, but which would not be very difficult to figure out. All this information kept coming to me through acquaintances after we had stopped writing to each other. I learned that he passed himself off as a single man but that, if anyone asked him about me, he would say that I was well off in Argentina and would soon be back with him.

During a trip to Israel he suffered a heart attack and had to return to Germany, where he was fitted with a pacemaker. He recovered shortly afterward and, instead of leading a quieter life considering his health problem, persisted in his excesses with women, and especially with alcohol.

A month before he died, Oskar had decided to return to Argentina, but his latest lover refused, perhaps fearing he might return to me.

I think I would not have taken him back. When I learned of his death through B'nai B'rith, Oskar had already been dead for me for a long time. Actually, it was he who killed himself in me with his indifference and his lack of affection.

Up until my trip to Germany in March 1995, I was convinced that Oskar had died of a heart attack. I was then told, however, that he had not survived an operation to replace his pacemaker. I was informed that he died in the operating room of a clinic in the city of Rüdesheim in 1974.

I later heard rumors that the surgeon in charge of the operation was the husband of one of his lovers. I cannot press charges—I don't even want to allow myself the suspicion—

but the situation is, to say the least, peculiar: a defenseless man places his life in the hands of a potential enemy. . . . Perhaps in some way, it was Oskar's last flirtation with danger.

A mass in his honor was held at the cathedral in Frankfurt. Rizyard Rechen, who had driven the truck when we fled Brünnlitz, arranged to have Oskar's body transferred to the Jerusalem cemetery, thus carrying out his last wish: to be buried in Jewish ground.

Just over thirty-seven years after he left, I was able to visit his tomb, thanks to Spielberg's film. I never imagined that this is how we would meet again: with him dead, and me an old lady who had to be taken there in a wheelchair.

I went up to his gravestone and repeated what the others had done: I placed a pebble on his tomb and silently said to him:

Well, Oskar, at last we meet again, but this is not the time for reproaches and complaints. It would not be fair to you or to me. Now you are in another world, in eternity, and I can no longer ask you all those questions to which in life you would have given evasive replies . . . and death is the best evasion of all. I have received no answer, my dear, I do not know why you abandoned me. . . . But what not even your death or my old age can change is that we are still married, this is how we are before God. I have forgiven you everything, everything. . . .

Murmuring these words, I let them push my wheelchair up the slight incline leading to the gravestone that marks the place where his remains are laid to rest, outside the Jewish cemetery of Jerusalem. I knew that somehow the power of my thoughts had reached him, and felt, after all those years, a strange inner peace filling my spirit.

Ready to Board

MONDAY, FEBRUARY 6, 1995. THIS YEAR WE ARE HAVING A strange summer. On a given day the temperature may go from one hundred to fifty degrees Fahrenheit, while a storm seems to divide the sky in half. I try to laugh at this absurd weather, but my health is affected by so many changes, and I have to stay in bed. Yesterday my right foot seemed to be paralyzed, and every step I took was terribly painful.

To keep busy when I am unable to do housework, I indulge in my favorite pastimes: reading the newspaper and listening to the news on the radio. I don't know why I persist; today, like most other days, seems to be filled with disasters. Could it be that so many catastrophic events make us feel less miserable? I was involved in an overwhelming, never-ending, hard-to-explain tragedy. But nobody seems to have learned anything from it. Death and destruction keep spreading all over the world like a plague.

I lived through the tragedy of war and would like my words to reach all those misguided souls who believe that hatred and death can solve problems. The opposite is true; everything is lost: love, affection, dignity. . . . Things that can never be recovered.

When people compliment me for what Oskar and I did, when I receive medals from governments and embassies, I feel like asking if it should not be everyone's obligation to save another's life, regardless of his or her color, race, nationality, or religion.

My mind is full of bitter memories. On the fiftieth anniversary of the liberation of the Auschwitz prisoners, my skin helplessly tensed up, and I felt a terror running through that, in spite of all these years, is a presence that never fades far away. Because there, according to the horrible Nazi statistics, one million, one hundred thousand human beings lost their lives, most of them Jews.

I read these numbers in books, and in spite of my having been so close, of having felt the echoes of the terror, it still seems utterly incomprehensible to me. That is why I think the act of forgiveness is so magnificent. It requires us at once to understand and to not forget, to value life and at the same time to not abandon the memory of those who died or the passion for justice.

To Love and to Curse

MARCH OF 1995 MARKED THE BEGINNING OF ONE OF THE MOST important trips of my life. I was to meet the Holy Father in Rome. My schedule included an audience with the Pope and then a meeting with the Grand Rabbi of Rome. Afterward, I would travel to Bonn, invited by the German government, for an interview with President Roman Herzog and with Rita Süssmuth, president of the German parliament. Just imagine, a peasant like me talking with some of the most influential people in the world. I already had the experience of meeting Bill Clinton, but this was very different because now I was the only guest of honor.

I could not, however, stop worrying about my health. It was a long trip, and my agenda was a busy one. But I still had a few days to get ready and leave everything in order at home.

For some years now I have had a young man named Leandro working for me; he does the shopping, takes care of the garden, and accompanies me whenever I have to go out because I am afraid to walk alone in the street. My legs can give out at any time. Once in a while they are so painful that I don't know whether to cry or to curse. . . .

Since in all truth I am a bit sick of crying, I swear, remembering cusswords in German, which happily very few people in Argentina understand. I find relief in lashing out and cursing, though of course this does not heal me.

Unfortunately, the press broke the news that I was going to visit the Pope, and that started a constant procession at my house of people who wanted to send him something, a book, a letter, a family relic. There was even someone who wanted me to tell John Paul II that his dead mother appeared to him in his dreams. The telephone did not stop ringing with similar requests. I tried to explain to everybody that what they were asking of me was not feasible, and I also felt that, aside from wasting my time, I was losing my patience. I was getting so upset that more than once I swore at those who intended to use me as a papal courier.

At last my day of departure came. I got up earlier than usual, went to the kitchen, and made myself a good cup of coffee, black as night, hot as hell, and sweet as love. I remembered Oskar, but the image that kept coming up was of him leaving. It made me so mad that I spilled half my coffee, which was indeed as hot as hell, on my nightgown.

Oskar was still much on my mind, and I didn't like this at all. I wanted to make this trip simply as Emilie. I couldn't tell then what it was I hated more: Oskar, or myself for being unable to expel him from my mind.

I decided to concentrate on what I had to do and put the past aside. I opened my closet and chose the things I wanted to take with me: a black dress with white stripes, given to me in Miami; two dress suits, a very elegant blue blouse, and a black coat purchased especially for this trip, plus a small suitcase, which I had no difficulty in filling.

The road to the Ezeiza airport was backed up. I felt a certain urgency to get there, although I had more than enough time. I usually can't stand the idea of having too much time.

A reporter asked me then what my future plans were. I simply answered:

"Young people should not die, but the old ones must."

Yes, it's that simple. It is pointless to make any plans when you are eighty-seven. Tomorrow may never come when you are as old as I am.

During the trip memories of Oskar again overwhelmed me. Until when, Oskar? Weren't our years together enough? How long does love last? Is passion a place you cannot leave behind until you die?

The Eternal City

I TRAVELED TO ROME WITH ERIKA ROSENBERG, WHO PERSUADED me to write this book. When we arrived at Fiumicino airport, a crowd of reporters was waiting for me with a deluge of the usual questions, and many others, not totally unpredictable: "How long will you be with us?" "Where will you be staying, Signora Schindler?" "Did you get to divorce your husband?"

Nobody seemed to realize that they were facing an old woman exhausted after a long journey. They wanted to know everything on the spot at once, in order to move on to something else. I consciously replied in monosyllables. I only wanted to get out of there as soon as possible. Fortunately, Erika decided to take me by the arm and pull me away, calling the press off. We got into a dark Lancia, which quickly took us to our hotel.

I looked through the window, trying to remember what I had learned about Rome in school at Alt Moletein, but the only thing that came to mind was the cracked voice of my history professor, too far removed in time for me to be able to listen to it again. In a second, I decided to ask the taxi driver about everything we were seeing. The man, dressed in a dark suit and looking more like an executive than a driver, answered all my questions in a friendly and knowledgeable manner. He told me a few things about Rome, which little by little I was beginning to remember. The good man, moreover, amazingly remembered the name of every single church we passed by, not a small feat considering there are more than six hundred of them in Rome.

We stayed at the Albergo d'Inghilterra, on Bocca di Leone Street. Our room was beautiful, its decor magnificent and austere at the same time. Over the headboard of the bed, I was welcomed by a delicate portrait of the Virgin Mary with Baby Jesus in her arms, which brought me back to the time in my adolescence that I spent at the convent school. Again I saw, as if far away, my small body kneeling and praying to God, asking Him for things that would never happen. . . .

In the room everything had a solemn aura, as if my visit with the Holy Father was totally pervasive.

The next morning I woke up at six, as usual. Still in bed, I again checked my schedule: at eleven, the audience with John Paul II; at one, a press conference at the Argentinean embassy to the Vatican.

Completely ignoring my travel discomforts, I walked up to the window and opened it wide.

There, before my eyes, were the famous Roman reddish slate roofs and, farther down, balconies with many-colored flowers. The sun shone brightly in a pure blue sky, filling the morning with light. Spring was at its peak, and I felt there was some truth in the old saying "All roads lead to Rome."

Quo Vadis?

AFTER A PEACEFUL BREAKFAST, WE LEFT THROUGH THE MAIN door, where a black limousine was waiting to take us to the

Vatican. Before getting into the luxurious car, I noticed a poster that read "Horaz Sienkiewicz, Polish writer, author of the book *Quo Vadis*."

I did not know why the sign was there, but it plunged me into dark reflection. It seemed that my entire life had been a constant questioning: *Quo Vadis?*—Where are you going, Emilie? It started at least as far back as Deutschbrod, where I had to throw away my passport to save my life. One day I had to take a ship to travel to a foreign country, and now here I was, after a long plane trip, before the doors of the Vatican for an interview with the Pope, no less. Were those two women, the one from before and this one, the same person?

The limo stopped abruptly and brought me back to earth. This time I was perfectly well aware of where I was going, though I could never have imagined it. My soul was at peace, and I felt that the beauty of the city and the flowering of spring were part of my personal celebration.

Suddenly the imposing dome of Saint Peter's Basilica rose before us. The faithful filled the street, young and old, standing or sitting on the pavement, all waiting for John Paul II to come out. We crossed the square and entered a corridor with benches, where we had to wait for almost an hour until the Holy Father showed up, flanked by his priest council and cardinals.

The Pope wore a red robe with a black sash because it was Lent. His retinue dressed in black cassocks with crossed red bands on the chest. John Paul II stood in front of me while I rose and looked into his deep blue eyes.

He raised his hand and blessed me, touching my head. Paralyzed and shaking with emotion, I wanted to say something but could not utter a word. Then he spoke to me in perfect German:

"I know who you are very well, and I am very grateful for what you have done. In Poland, especially in the Cracow region, many Polish Jews were saved thanks to you and your husband, but your example of solidarity also saved Polish Catholics."

He added that the country of his birth felt a great deal of respect and affection for me. I gave him a parchment invitation to the opening of a hall, named after Oskar and me, at the Argentinean House in Jerusalem. He looked at it and continued walking toward another group of people, leaving behind a memory that will be with me until the day I die.

When we left the Holy See, it was very windy. My hair was ruffled, and I tried to straighten it with my fingers. In my hands I tried to find the traces of the papal blessing.

A Brand on the Skin

NO LESS MOVING WAS THE MEETING WITH THE GRAND RABBI of Rome, home to about thirty-five thousand of the sixty thousand Jews who live throughout Italy.

A fairly old man dressed entirely in gray approached me, hat in hand. He had rolled up his left sleeve to display, with a mixture of pride and sadness, the numbers that the Nazis had branded on his skin. He had been through three concentration camps—Auschwitz, Dachau, and Treblinka—and had survived thanks to his willpower and God's help.

After saying this, he took me by the arm and helped me enter the synagogue. The history of the Holocaust was evident everywhere, refusing to die. The man's presence brought me back to Plaschow, the SS, Amon Goeth. . . . Having met the executioners at close quarters, I could have an understanding of how it must have been for the victims in the concentration camps. To compare the Nazis to animals is not useful at all in trying to understand the cruelty of which they were capable. They were Evil in its most perfect and absolute form, something that has nothing to do with nature, but rather with the most infamous and brutal corners of the human soul.

The Grand Rabbi gave me a magnificent reception. He presented me with two beautiful books on the history of Italian Jews, and then brought me to a drawing room decorated with old scrolls and scriptures, in the center of which a huge wooden candelabrum with seven candles rested on a round table. His words, evoking the war years, managed to reach deep into my soul.

Dazed by a strange mixture of emotions and happiness, I decided to get out of the car at the Piazza Spagna and walk the two remaining blocks to the hotel.

At noon on the following day, we left the hotel and explored the streets, which in such a short time seemed familiar. Everything in Rome was gentle, the climate, the city, and especially the people, so open and friendly.

An unpleasant surprise, however, was waiting for us at the airport. That same morning, the porters had gone on strike. Luckily, we finally found someone to help us, but the nervousness caused by the situation had left me utterly exhausted. All the emotions of the meetings with the Pope and the Grand Rabbi, the walk in the city, and the harassing by reporters turned out to be too much for me.

Almost out of breath, I boarded the Lufthansa airplane that would take us to Frankfurt. The captain's voice, addressing the passengers in German, was reassuring. It was like recovering something familiar, intimate. . . . The plane departed a few minutes later, flying over some of Rome's suburbs. Seeing the world from up there fascinates me, and whenever I fly, I try to get a window seat. Everything gets smaller, the cities seem like doll houses, and the rivers like lines drawn with a dark pencil on a multicolored map. All sense of time and space vanishes.

I saw the Alps again when the plane crossed the border. I had seen them last with Oskar, on the overland trip from Munich to Genoa to board the ship that was to take us to Argentina.

The Taste of Snow

AT THE COLOGNE-BONN AIRPORT WE WERE MET BY A YOUNG lady with blond hair and a cream-colored dress, who in a soft and almost timid voice asked me if I was Frau Schindler. It was Julia Pabsch, daughter of the German ambassador to Buenos Aires. She said she would take care of us during our stay in Bonn.

We got into a black Mercedes and after a half-hour trip arrived at the Bristol Hotel, which impressed me with its elegant entrance and its red carpet leading to two restaurants, and to a spacious foyer. Everything looked so open and comfortable that I joyfully looked forward to our week-long stay.

The first thing people in Bonn do is remind tourists that they are in Beethoven's birthplace. I was no exception to the rule and took due note. However, when it came to historical and geographical information, I fell happily asleep. Thank God an old lady is forgiven for nearly anything, and my lack of courtesy was almost received with approval. To fall asleep in a place is a way of showing one feels comfortable there, isn't it?

The following day was cold and windy. Spring seemed to be a privilege reserved for the Romans. In Bonn nobody appeared even to have noticed the change in season. When I sat down at the breakfast table loaded with delicacies, I remembered the relief packages we used to receive at Regensburg after the war. It seemed incredible how much everything had changed in only fifty years. The waitress came and, with a smile, said these not unexpected, but magical words:

"Guten Morgen, Frau Schindler."

It was the first "good morning" in my native language I had heard in many years. It sounded strange and pleasant, like a melody from an old recording, dusty and forgotten.

When I stepped out of the hotel, it was snowing. Almost fifty years living in a corner of the world where snow is unknown had made me forget its texture, that delightful coldness that melts in your hands. I caught a flake and took it to my mouth. Here was the taste of my childhood: Christmas, the walks through the woods blanketed in white, the big snowballs we made for our great battles with Rita Gross and our other friends. My brother always managed to win in the end, and I would withdraw to a corner without completely admitting defeat, repeating to myself: "We are beaten but not conquered, in this battle nobody dies." A tenet I would put into practice for the rest of my life.

Meeting Traude Again

A GREAT EMOTIONAL MOMENT AWAITED ME IN BONN THE DAY after my arrival: my niece Traude, whom I had not seen since leaving Europe, would come to see me with her husband.

They lived near Munich, and I decided to meet them at the station. I remember it was very cold on the platform, and the loudspeakers announced that the train was delayed thirty minutes. Although warmly dressed, I could not help shivering. And I saw myself again in Constance, in an almost summery dress and terribly hungry, by the very same river that flows past Bonn, awaiting only God knows what.

Suddenly two figures on the platform came running and

shouting, "Aunt Millie, Aunt Millie!" It was Traude and her husband, Nini. They were hugging me before I could straighten my hair to look more presentable. After so many years without seeing each other, we were speechless. We could not take our eyes off each other, but we could not utter a word, though we both had so much to say. Only our eyes were doing the talking.

I recognized in Traude the sweet girl I had raised and spoiled as if she were my own. Time, of course, had also left its marks on her, but her eyes and her laughter were still as bright and totally charming. She will always be my little girl. In spite of the distance, I never stopped thinking of her. I often wondered what she was doing, what her life was like, and whether she remembered her aunt Emilie.

When Traude found out about my trip to Germany, she phoned and told me she would come visit me wherever I might be. . . . And there she was, with her green coat and huge smile, repeating my name over and over again.

While we had something hot to drink in an old-style café with very white walls, mirrored doors, and red velvet armchairs, my niece pulled out of her handbag a package of family photos.

"They are from the album you gave me at Brünnlitz," Traude said with tears in her eyes. "I have treasured them all this time. They are yours, Aunt Emilie."

Those photographs were the only existing testimony of my family, my childhood, my years with Oskar. . . . They had survived the catastrophe, thanks to Traude. When the Russian troops came, my niece was with her mother and her two younger brothers, Klaus and Elli. A soldier knocked on the door and ordered them out, hands up. Traude, unwilling to let go of that treasure, ran and grabbed the album. It was too big and did not fit under her clothes, so she tore out the pictures and hid them under her pullover.

It got late, and we were still in that old-style café holding hands. We looked at the photos together and remembered small anecdotes that photos could not tell.

"Remember, Aunt Millie, the night you wanted to go to the movies with Uncle Oskar, and I insisted on going with you, no matter how many times you said you would not take me? You finally got so mad that you spanked me twice on my behind."

We laughed, remembering her pranks. As a child, Traude could try the patience of a saint. Now she had changed into an intelligent and wise woman, the wife of a handsome Italian engineer and mother of a twenty-six-year-old daughter. In spite of the years, she had not lost her marvelous sense of humor and, deep down, still was to all those around her that beautiful, flirtatious little girl, seductive and irresistible like Oskar.

With those photographs Traude gave me back an important part of my life. That is why I included them here, to share them with you. You can look at them and again find my life's story. If you look closely, it's all there, complete, without any lies.

A Visit to the President

A SNOWSTORM WAS AN APPROPRIATE ENDING FOR THOSE COLD and happy days. The flakes settled on the rooftops, and the trees acquired a white and festive cover that the wind would whirl away in every direction. The weather did not encourage any outings, but I knew President Roman Herzog was waiting for me at eight-thirty. I was so anxious and excited that I skipped breakfast and went to my appointment with nothing but black coffee and a tranquilizer.

The place where I was to meet President Roman Herzog

was not far from the hotel. The car took an avenue parallel to the Rhine, whose dark and gloomy waters reminded me of the German song:

Ich weiss nicht, was soll es bedeuten,
Dass ich so traurig bin;
Ein Märchen aus uralten Zeiten,
Das kommt mir nicht aus dem Sinn.

[I do not know the meaning of my great sadness;
an ancient legend keeps haunting my mind.]

I hummed "Die Lorelei" without the words, a little out of tune. Erika looked amused; she had never heard me sing. Shortly afterward, we arrived at the government building, where we were welcomed by an official who took us to a long hall, its walls covered with paintings. It was not a very pleasant place, perhaps a bit too solemn. But luckily, President Herzog was not solemn. He asked no questions about the war and did not pry into my life. He inquired about my health and made a few comments, sounding official at times and witty at others, regarding the Order of Merit that the German embassy of Buenos Aires had bestowed upon me and that I wore especially for the occasion. He also spoke of his family life and his childhood in Bavaria.

Herzog impressed me as being a good man, aware of how tired I was of digging into the past. Being sensitive, that's what it is, something I miss a lot. . . . Perhaps this was Oskar's greatest virtue and the secret of his irresistible seductiveness.

The trip back to the hotel was a lot less pleasant. The many pills I took to soothe the pain in my bones had upset my stomach, and on top of it, my bones still ached. This was how I started my return voyage to Argentina, my second home.

My Photo

AS SOON AS I GOT BACK TO SAN VICENTE, I WENT TO MY ROOM, determined to place my head on the pillow and fall into a deep sleep right away.

I put on my nightgown and went to bed. On my night table was a German magazine with a story on Emilie Schindler. Without too much interest in the character, I started to leaf through the pages and found a huge photograph of that old lady.

Seeing my picture there made me want to read the article. Under the bedside lamp the wrinkles on Emilie's face grew even bigger, spreading all over her face: her cheeks, forehead, eyelids; it looked like a spider's web spun in haste. . . . And that old lady is me, I thought. How old, how terribly old! That photo was the summary of my life. I cried and laughed at the same time. I realized that each wrinkle was like a line in the book of my life, and time had not been its only author.

Epilogue

A Toast to Life

WELL, I DON'T THINK I HAVE ANYTHING ELSE TO SAY.
Now you know everything about Emilie, her
childhood, her first and only love, Schindler's list,
her life after the war, her leaving for Argentina.
Now you know her soul, her joys, and her sorrows.

In these pages I decided to come out of the
shadows, and I have taken pains to throw as
much light as possible on the past. I have done so
from this corner of the world, seemingly so far
away, where I live surrounded by dogs and cats
that cannot speak but are great company. Let's
remember that words are the only opposite of
silence: the old German words, which I used to
write this book, words that I kept rediscovering
little by little in the recesses of my weary memory.

It is really wonderful. . . . When I started writing, I never thought that the memories of so many
events had remained locked in my mind. Emilie
turned out better than I had thought, after all. I
often feared that when getting to the last chapter
of my memoirs, everything would be colored by
some of the bitterness and despair of farewells.
But that's not the way it is, nor does it have to be.

I had the good fortune of being able to help people beset by tragedy, and I believe I have contributed, to the best of my ability, to making this world a better place in which to live.

To reencounter the hardworking Emilie who haggled on the black market, who used to walk from one corner of the Brünnlitz factory to the other, and who harbored a secret hatred for the Nazis, helped make me realize that, in spite of all my mistakes, my life has not been in vain. The fact that you are reading these last lines confirms this.

The moral of my story is simple: a fellow human being always has the right to life. Like so many others during the war, I think I have experienced in my own flesh that "Love one another" is not an empty phrase but a maxim worth living by, even in the worst of circumstances. The descendants of those on Schindler's list have shown this to be true: they are living, having children, remembering. . . .

To love one another. That is life, such as I had learned since early childhood: to love, and to struggle. . . . I have written this book in the hope that it will be of use to others, because it is others who give meaning to our acts. As on the evening I decided to write my memoirs, I again lift my glass to celebrate and give thanks to God.

A toast to all of you, my fellow human beings. I hope that as you close this book, you will want to make a toast for my husband. . . . And for me, too.